I've Got a

SECRET

ARMOR
BOOKS

Kimberlee Stone

I've Got A Secret by Kimberlee Stone

Published by: Armor Books
P.O. Box 1050
Lawrenceville, GA 30046
www.armorbooks.com

First Printing: September 2002

Unless otherwise noted, all Scripture quotations are from the Holy Bible, New International Version. Copyright © 1973, 1978, 1984, International Bible Society. Used by permission.

International Standard Book Number: 1-55829-225-X

02 03 04 05 06   8 7 6 5 4 3 2 1
Printed in the United States of America

Contents

For Sophia,
Girl of my dreams.

Prologue

Maybe it was the moon, the way its slant of white light cradled her face and danced off the walls to create a nightlight more splendid than any other I had ever seen.

Or maybe it was the perfect ending to the perfect day that made me want to turn back the hands on the clock so I wouldn't miss a single breath while she slept. Nevertheless, I knelt on the floor next to my daughter and invited myself into her dreams while the moon gazed down at us. Something unseen, but not unfelt, made me linger in Sophia's room when there were clothes to be folded and dishes to be put away.

Okay, maybe the day wasn't ideal. Perhaps I raised my voice one too many times or rattled off idle threats about what I was going to do if she put one more dirty penny into her mouth. Somehow though the very act of watching my daughter sleep evoked a calm that stilled my racing heart while gratitude to God washed over me. He had supplied the perfect ending to a long journey.

I wonder how I can be so grateful on one hand

yet feel a surge of hopelessness rising from some unknown crevasse, as it did before. Immediately I try to put that feeling back into its box and convince myself I am a different person than I was twenty months ago. Right?

In a feeble attempt to piece the puzzle of my life together, I come up short. Something is missing, like the corner puzzle piece that falls between the couch cushions and keeps me from completing the picture displayed on the box cover. I feel oddly incomplete tonight.

What do these next few months hold? Another child? Please, God, another child! Blood quickens its course through my veins at the very thought that God could be so good to enlarge our family. How He will do that is part of the mystery. I hardly have the strength to go through another adoption; I still cannot understand why we've been chosen for this lot in life, why having children is so difficult. How much easier it would be for God to allow me to conceive! No more profiles to create, home studies to complete or months to wait. Does God truly carve out a path such as mine, with more twists and bends in it than I can keep up with? Yet looking at this tiny human being curled up between the covers, I realize with certainty that there must be a divine plan to the journey that brought me to this place—being someone's mommy.

Softly as a whisper, I hear God. Maybe not audibly, but in the depth of my heart where only I can hear. And tonight, beside Sophia's bed, I am listening.

"If it weren't for you, she would never know Me. She would never know the promise of Heaven."

Suddenly everything makes sense. I feel different, lighter, as if something has been lifted. It doesn't take long to realize that my questions, my fears, are gone. The long days and nights spent in the desert, where only my tears were familiar, is a mere step. A step made for exactly this moment in my life. A step not unlike the voyage that led me to this very moment.

February 1995

Today I found a cheap paper calendar buried beneath a pile of junk. I dusted it off, scanned its unmarked pages, and contemplated throwing it into the garbage. Calendars are of no use to me halfway through the year. Besides, I end up losing them or simply get tired of them. Then it hit me—this calendar is going to help me have a baby.

With the number "1995" emblazoned before my face, the finality of years gone by echoes in my mind. I can't believe Regi and I have been married for over five years now. How quickly the years have escaped us. I remember the day two unsuspecting people in their twenties walked down the aisle and joined lives, unaware that life wouldn't always be so sensational. Marriage is wonderful, all that I expected, but something is missing. I believe I've come up with the missing link too. Children.

Five years is a nice round number of years to get to know each other. We have experienced job changes, location changes, and changes in each other that have reshaped our existence. Our desires are different from when we first married, and what comes second nature to me usually turns out to be second nature to Regi. We are a pretty good partnership.

10

I don't know how to approach him about my desire to start a family. We don't discuss it ever, and although I know he loves children, I wonder if he has conditioned himself against their demanding needs. We aren't using any birth control and I quietly hold out hope that one of these months I'll get pregnant.

That's where this little calendar comes in. I think I'll start keeping track of my cycle in order to figure out when the best time for me to get pregnant will be. This could be construed as deceptive, but worse could happen. We'll see how the months pan out.

The Effects of Abortion

March 1995

My little calendar has proven beneficial. I don't hide the calendar but I do have my own secret code that Regi would never suspect at first glance. Tiny dots and capital letters all have their meaning that only I can figure out. I am a secret agent engaged on a highly confidential mission.

May 1995

March and April have passed and of course I'm not pregnant. I certainly never intended to be, although my calendar helps put things into perspective. Regi is slowly letting his guard down although I don't say anything about my desires. Whenever the time is appropriate, I will bring up the issue of having a baby and see how it flies.

The wish to have children doesn't come from unhappiness with my life. Actually, it seems the logical next step for two people to take when sharing their lives. I sense Regi's hesitation but don't understand it. He reasons that time with a baby will take the place of "our time." I, on the month with one thing on my mind: getting pregnant. It is becoming a burning obsession, and I don't like how these feelings leave me reeling with frustration. I'm beginning to wonder if I even deserve to be pregnant, although I share that with no one.

Eight years ago I found out I was pregnant. For a nineteen-year-old, this was the worst possible news. In my second year of college, I was about to leave home to complete my junior and senior years at a state university, and I couldn't change my plans. I convinced myself I was too young to give up my future dreams and in no way ready to be married. Too young to be in an immoral relationship, I certainly never considered the possibility of consequences to my actions.

I remember hanging out with the popular crowd at school and how I made good grades. Drinking alcohol started in high school, usually on Friday nights after football games with friends. It started slowly, first by holding a beer bottle just to fit in, then by taking a few sips to look like I enjoyed it, then ultimately developing a taste for it. When you try something often enough, it becomes appetizing. Peer pressure was difficult to overcome, and while no one forced me to my demise, I followed the actions of those around me.

Real life doesn't withhold itself from kids who

other hand, think a baby will complement that time. I would never tell him that I think he enjoys still being a kid and likes the ability to be irresponsible in some ways. I don't know how we'll ever agree on this issue, especially when he is a vital part in this whole baby-making process!

July 1995

Still not pregnant. It is truly a hit or miss thing, especially since I'm the only one purposefully trying here. I'm not aching for a child at this point, but the desire grows daily.

Many of my friends have babies, and what beautiful changes have taken place in their lives. Watching a man and wife suddenly become part of a family is quite a blessing. My greatest joy is cuddling these fragile human beings and holding them close to my heart. People always spurt out comments like "You'll be next," which I take lightly and usually laugh off. Their words don't affect me nearly as much as having a husband who won't even discuss starting a family.

September 1995

The year is quickly coming to a halt, and my calendar reminds me of that daily. Time flies when you don't want it to! I wish I could take back many of those days and reshape them into better memories. It isn't easy living month to are raised in church, taught Bible verses, and sing songs like "Jesus Loves Me." Instead, souls like mine often find the battle against evil the hardest.

My "good" self constantly battled my "bad" self, and I became a master of charades. I kept Sunday mornings and Saturday nights separate–and managed to pull them off week after week. As long as I showed up for church, nobody asked any questions. Living this lifestyle was not easy, and living with myself was even harder. It caught up to me the day the sign turned positive on the home pregnancy test. My twin lives intersected, and I was ill–equipped to handle what was happening.

I don't know why the horror of my abortion haunts me now. I don't wake up in cold sweats or dream about that frightening day, but the issue of killing babies has taken up residence in my mind daily. Driving home from work the other day I heard a radio program discussing the pro-life vs. pro-choice debate. Feelings I thought were quashed came boiling to the surface. Especially since I wanted to jump on the bandwagon and cheer on the battle to save unborn lives. Me? What a hypocrite, I thought, and decided to distinguish whatever was brewing inside of me.

November 1995

Regi and I have talked about the issue of children but our discussions go nowhere. I wish

I knew the real reason for his hesitancy. Bad childhood? Bad adulthood? What could it be? Part of my problem is that I've watched too many romantic movies where the husband and wife pledge undying love. The man looks into the wife's eyes and says something silly like, "My darling, I long for you to be the mother of my children." Or, "Having children with you will complete my life." When will I wake up from this dream and realize I'm not living my life on the big screen?

The abortion issue, on the other hand, is out of control. I can't help but think God is bringing it to my mind for a reason. But why? I've prayed about it and wonder if He wants me to "come out of the closet" with my secret. The more I think about it, the more I know that is impossible. I long to confide in Regi but can't muster the courage. The only reason I want to tell him now is because I've recently started wondering if the abortion has something to do with my inability to get pregnant.

Regi and I have not been so careful lately. It's safe to say we are unofficially trying to have a baby. Though we've never spoken about it, I assume this is his way of saying he wouldn't be upset if I got pregnant. Now I look to my calendar religiously and pray every month that our efforts paid off. While it's exciting to hold out hope every month that I'm pregnant, it is also emotionally draining. I deal with all these issues alone, and it is difficult.

January 1996

The New Year has blown in like a tornado—what an opportunity to wipe the slate clean and start over.

I made it through the holidays without getting pregnant, and honestly I didn't think much about it. How freeing not to get my hopes up only to be dashed. This, however, was one of those months where I sensed, with no other leading but my own, that I was pregnant. I tried to convince myself one night that our attempt was successful, like God told me or something. For weeks I waited only to be frustrated when the signs rushed in.

I have started living month to month like this and am under stress such as I've never felt before. I'm trying to sort my feelings out about the abortion but am having a hard time at that. I remember when, months after the abortion, I was broken and weeping before God. The harsh reality of what I had done zeroed in on my daily existence, paralyzing me with remorse and shame. The forgiveness and freedom I felt from Christ was indeed life changing. At the moment He forgave and set me free, I started living a normal life again. I left my sin in His hands and haven't picked it up until now. Why do I feel the need to do so? Whatever the reason, I have this nagging sense that I need to confess to Regi, but I'm scared. I can't imagine what his reaction will be and have started to pray that God will work out the how's and when's. I am laden with fear that my day of judgment has finally come and I must tell Regi what worries me now more than anything. We will never have children because of my horrible past.

February 1996

I must learn not to ask something of the Lord if I don't really want an answer. Through a strange turn of events, the time has come for me to share everything with Regi. My abortion, my incredible desire to have children, my keeping track of trying to get pregnant. No holds barred.

How do I tell the person who thinks he knows me best about my shameful past? A past so embarrassing it will undoubtedly lower his opinion of me?

The time proved right when we were about thirty thousand feet in the air and on a trip. Strapped to our seats in the huge jet, I fidgeted so much he knew something was up. Knowing he couldn't run or yell comforted me somewhat, but that also meant I couldn't run or yell either. Quite calmly, I told him everything. His response was just what I expected—emotionless and devastating. But what a release for me! Suddenly I wanted to share months of pent up emotions with him. I would have had he not turned a deaf ear to me.

He clammed up and said he would deal with it in his own way. I figured he would ask all kinds of questions but he never did. Did I do the right thing? For a brief second I wanted to recapture those few moments and forget about telling him. If Regi wouldn't talk about having children with me, how did I expect him to ask about the child I didn't have?

He doesn't seem to realize the abortion could have something to do with us not getting pregnant. He probably never will. I vow to tuck the hurts deep in my heart and deal with them as I have until now—alone.

18

April 1996

While I abandoned my pen for a few months, my heart won't allow me that choice. Much has changed in our lives since the time I last wrote, but my dreams remain the same. They remain mine alone.

We just completed a major move in location and job, and now the newness is wearing off. I fully intend this to be a new start in a new community so I can start a new way of thinking. Not so much about yesterday's pain, but of new motivations, hobbies, and attitudes. A chance to stash the old me into a shoebox to be cataloged among the other dusty boxes in the attic.

Now that there are no more boxes to unpack and the phone hasn't started ringing with well-intentioned new friends, I have nothing to do but rekindle my past. I'm convinced that because of my sinful past, I will never find true peace. I do not deserve it.

I fantasize about living in a world where I take charge of my fears and face the dawn with strength. As surely as I take one step forward, I am knocked down by my subconscious that reminds me of my unresolved past. If I could just find the freedom to dance during the difficult times, I believe I would make it.

Ever since the moment I told Regi of my past, I can hardly get the abortion off my mind. It's been almost ten years since I terminated my pregnancy, yet the pain and shame are just now coming to life. While I do not deny its existence, I simply choose not to rehash that experience every day of my life. The pain will never be erased; the memory will never fade. Yet I'm determined to muster the strength to face my reflection in the mirror and walk through life one step at a time, regardless of the outcome.

I do not hate myself. I do not hate God. I hate what I did. I despise my lack of judgment, the inability to think for myself and how it would affect my future. I had the strength to turn and run, I just didn't act on it. I cried out to God, I just didn't listen. If only I knew the Lord then like I do now, everything would be different.

Today I am driven to think that no one has ever walked in my shoes or felt the penetrating loneliness that tugs at my heart for this child I never knew. If only there were someone I could talk to who had been through the horror of abortion. I know I'm not the only one who's afraid of confessing their ugly sins, afraid of how others will respond. People talk about a loving, forgiving God, but can they be like Him?

I am angry with myself for believing the pat explanation that I would heal in time and forget about the baby I destroyed. Well, here's a news flash: I cannot forget and will never forget, as long as I live. What they didn't tell me was how to cope and erase my memory. Where are they now?

The pain of my abortion has filled the spot where I left the pain of not being able to get pregnant. Somehow the two go hand-in-hand, but I can hardly deal with both at the same time. I've also been grieving the possibility that I'll never have a child. Not only because of my physical limitations but also because of Regi's nonexistent desire for a baby.

Years of pent up shame and guilt have brought me to what I have secretly known all along—that the abortion has scarred me, physically and emotionally. This generic fear lurks quietly and keeps me guessing as to when it will pop up again. Every time I make it through another day, I'm grateful. Then I put up my guard and wonder if tomorrow will be my day of reckoning.

For many years now I have blamed my inability to get pregnant on my abortion. If that suspicion is confirmed, I don't know how I'll hide behind this facade any longer. People will find out, they will judge, and I will wither away in self-pity. God has every right to dash my hopes of having a child, but I do not believe He operates that way. For every obstacle that has ever crossed my path, He has provided a way around.

21

Do I even have the right to long for new life inside of me again? The emptiness my arms feel in the early hours mirrors that of my empty belly. They both long to feel life squirming within.

Have I been abandoned by motherhood? The thought wages war within my mind, saying I am not worthy to be among those ranks. Satan constantly throws darts at my bravado, attempting to stake his claim over my soul for ending my pregnancy. His determination only fuels my desire to cling to God and search for goodness to come from this tragedy.

For as long as I can remember, I have wanted children—a lot of them. No career is appealing enough to lure me away from this calling.

Chocolate cookies and nap times rank above corporate lunches and business suits in my mind! I go to bed at night dreaming of what I will look like pregnant, appropriate names for a girl or boy, and what it will feel like walking into church for the first time with a new baby.

I am weary of this roller coaster every month as I silently hope I am pregnant. No one knows my feelings, and so I deal with the loss every month alone. I am so tired of having my hopes dashed every twenty-eight days. The truth is, in six years of marriage I have never been late; this month won't be any different. Nonetheless, I hope I messed up the days and counted wrong. Only when the signs unveil themselves and I am not pregnant do my emotions turn sour. I am angry at my youthful foolishness and curse the next few days of constant reminder that something must be wrong with me.

May 1, 1996

Talking about the abortion is not the hard part. Thinking about it is. When I am alone, I tiptoe around my emotions and scars. The shame of that day may never fully be erased, although I dream of that time.

Nearly ten years ago the doctor handed down my sentence: positive. He backed up what I already knew, though I privately held out hope that the home pregnancy test was wrong. Maybe I did just have the flu. I left the doctor's office alone that day and knew that was how I would face most of the ensuing days. I don't remember where the strength came from to face my parents morning after morning without breaking down and telling them I was pregnant, but I put on the show of my life.

One night after I went to bed my mother came and sat on the side of my bed to talk. I wanted so badly to tell her, but I couldn't. I simply could not allow my parents the humiliation and anger. I stuck to the philosophy that what they didn't know wouldn't hurt them.

23

I knew, as the day drew closer, that what I was about to do was wrong and that it grieved my heavenly Father. At the time, though, being pregnant was more devastating than having an abortion. My thoughts were skewed, my heart hardened. Instead of realizing my parents could have helped me, I decided to deal with my situation on my own.

My doctor was understanding, almost consolable, as if he were going to help me get over a common cold. In his defense, he encouraged me to tell my mother but never pushed the issue. He let me know, in no uncertain terms, that he could take care of it, quickly and quietly, as if it were no big deal.

The doctor and I arranged for the procedure to take place at the hospital, not one of those heavily picketed clinics where abortions are performed around the clock. It would be expensive, but I thought I would be spared further embarrassment and danger. How many other women had turned to this doctor who delivered babies on one day and killed them on others?

When the nurses and doctor wheeled me into the operating room, they were nonchalant. Did they think this was a routine procedure? The operating room was sterile, and my heart was no better. As the strange smell permeated my nostrils, I drifted off to sleep.

24

To this day I am most saddened by the realization that God never left my side during the whole procedure. I would like to think He turned His head, or left me alone until the end. Anything so He didn't have to endure my shame. Yet, at the same time, I think how wonderful it is to know He never runs away during the bad times.

O Lord, you have searched me and you know me. You know when I sit and when I rise; you perceive my thoughts from afar. You discern my going out and my lying down; you are familiar with all my ways. Before a word is on my tongue you know it completely, O Lord. You hem me in—behind and before; you have laid your hand upon me. Such knowledge is too wonderful for me, too lofty for me to attain. Where can I go from your Spirit?

Where can I flee from your presence? If I go up to the heavens, you are there; if I make my bed in the depths, you are there. If I rise on the wings of the dawn, if I settle on the far side of the sea, even there your hand will guide me, your right hand will hold me fast. If I say, "Surely the darkness will hide me and the light become night around me," even the darkness will not be dark to you; the night will shine like the day, for darkness is as light to you. —Psalm 139:1-12, NIV

About a year after my abortion, I could not live with myself any longer. I felt so shameful and thought the Lord didn't love me anymore. I cried out to Him, first for forgiveness, then for mercy that I wouldn't be reminded daily of what I did. At that moment I felt a supernatural wave of new life sweep over me as the weight of my sin was lifted. I knew that God had mercifully erased the pain and guilt from my heart and mind. I knew that I would never forget what I had done, but with God's help I could start anew from that moment on. The power of God healed my heart in ways I never could.

25

Dealing With Infertility

May 10, 1996

It is my decision to go in search of some answers. I am certain that now is the time to find out what the problem is and tackle it head on. I have made a doctor's appointment and plan to lay my cards on the table. If something is wrong with me, at least I will know how to pray. I've always thought that people would conjure their own reasons for my infertility and force me to reveal my past. Will they know I did something wrong when I was a teenager? Do I really want to know if I have ruined my chances to conceive? Even if it means a negative outcome, my need to know wins out.

I don't know how to tell Regi about my secret agenda for fear that he will not support my efforts. He won't stop me, but he may dampen my spirits. I still long for him to want a baby, but cannot and will not force the issue. I place it in God's hands and pray that He changes Regi's heart and we get through this whole situation. At least I'm doing something to get to the bottom of these problems;

I actually look forward to knowing more. Until then, I'll face each day and dream of a child to call my own.

May 23, 1996

I skimmed through the Yellow Pages to find one of those Christian crisis pregnancy centers that claimed they could help girls in trouble. Do people really look in the Yellow Pages for help when they are pregnant and have nowhere else to turn? Sounds pretty ridiculous but it was a place to start. I have decided to do something constructive with my abortion, and all I can think of is becoming a volunteer and saving the lives of other unborn babies. How many crisis counselors can say they've actually had an abortion and tell young women how it messed up their lives?

27

I called the first one I came to. As I inquired about the agency and asked all kinds of questions, I knew I had found my calling. Going through volunteer counseling training sounded like a challenge, but it would help open the lines of communication in talking about my own abortion. As I talked to the woman at the agency, I knew it wouldn't be fair not to tell her about my abortion, so I did. I was shocked when she responded that she too had an abortion in her past along with many of their other volunteers. Imagine my surprise and the humility that swept over me. I thought I would be their first!

I cannot fully explain the feeling I had toward the stranger on the other end of the line. I had finally told someone about my past and wasn't condemned; I felt an instant kinship. She went on to say that potential volunteers who have had an abortion are required to go through the agency's thirteen-week post-abortion Bible study. I pretended to be interested, but I knew I would never go through with such a step. What if someone knew me? And what could there possibly be to talk about since my abortion happened so many years ago? I had resolved all the issues within myself, without any assistance, and didn't need anyone probing around looking for some emotion!

When the woman asked, I gave her my address so she could send me some information. But I plan to throw it away when it arrives in the mail. Besides, Regi will think I've lost all my common sense!

May 26, 1996

But you are a shield around me, O Lord;
you bestow glory on me and lift up my head.
—Psalm 3:3, NIV

Today I'm convinced that I am pregnant. I can't wait to square off with the twenty-eighth day of this month to see who wins. This is my way of stepping out in faith and believing I have overcome my obstacle of infertility. I should have had such bold faith months ago!

What would I do if I found out tomorrow that I could never have a child? Would it change anything? Would God become smaller and my pursuit of Him lessen? I remind myself of my ultimate reason for living—to serve God. I was made in His image, allowed grace through His Son, and created to worship Him. Whether or not a child comes from my body, bears my resemblance, or wears my name does not distinguish who I am in Christ. While I have come to that realization today, I am merely human. In all likelihood I will forget my newfound revelation and rumble with fear again.

My subconscious will not leave me alone! These past three nights I've dreamed about babies, last night one of my own. I desperately try not to create false illusions of motherhood, but these dreams keep coming. Of course, until I am proven wrong, I take them as signs from God telling me I am pregnant. I want so much to believe.

I think about what His word says in Psalm 3:3. If not for His redeeming grace, I could not enter into His presence and find peace and rest. The moment I step out of His presence, my thoughts are heavy with questions, so I try to stay in an attitude of worship that gives me the strength I need to face another day.

How thankful I am that God is willing to welcome me when I seek Him. He is quick to replace my sorrow with joy, my unbelief with hope, my emptiness with fullness.

May 27, 1996

> Answer me when I call to you, O my righteous God. Give me relief from my distress; be merciful to me and hear my prayer. How long, O men, will you turn my glory into shame? How long will you love delusions and seek false gods? Know that the Lord has set apart the godly for himself; the Lord will hear when I call to him. In your anger do not sin; when you are on your beds, search your hearts and be silent. Offer right sacrifices and trust in the Lord. Many are asking, "Who can show us any good?" Let the light of your face shine upon us, O Lord. You have filled my heart with greater joy than when their grain and new wine abound. I will lie down and sleep in peace, for you alone, O Lord, make me dwell in safety.
>
> —Psalm 4, NIV

The days continue to pass, slowly. Still no signs. I try not to get excited, although it's difficult. I think it has been more than twenty-eight days, which means I am late—a good sign.

Every now and then I feel a cramp in my stomach. At its onset, disappointment blankets my spirit like an early morning fog. I will wait one more day and try to rest my mind. I am exhausted from too much thinking.

May 28, 1996

Finding out I'm not pregnant comes as no surprise. It hurts the most after I have conjured up the absurd notion that our efforts at conception won out. I wince when the evidence appears and am further convinced that something is definitely wrong with me.

My faith is dwindling, and I don't know how I can face another month of feeling depressed and abandoned by God. I thought faith meant believing wholeheartedly about something, but now I consider it to be a hyped-up emotion that people talk about only after something good has happened.

Today I fight the tears. If I start to cry, it will be impossible to stop. It would be easier to curl up beneath my comforter and sleep for days, far away from God, the world, and even myself. The silence around me must mean God has forgotten. I try to find a comforting thought or hear Him amidst the confusion, but He seems so far away.

May 31, 1996

I received an unmarked package in the mail today and tore it open in hopes that it was a gift from a long lost friend or something else to cheer me up. It wasn't. The package contained information sheets and brochures on the post-abortion Bible study group. I never intended to look at this stuff, let alone read through it, for fear the contents may interest me. Yet every time I put the papers down I was drawn to pick them up again. Something inside me struck a chord with the words that spoke of healing, depression and guilt, letting go. I could relate to every word written in the pages. Reluctantly, I realize I haven't successfully dealt with my abortion. Not to this extent anyway.

For the first time all week, I want to go through with the Bible study. I don't know why, but I can't resist the urge. The only thing that holds me back is the fear that someone might know me, or know someone from my church. I am certainly not ready to share this with anyone and don't know how private these Bible studies are.

When I told Regi about my phone call to the crisis pregnancy center and my interest in the Bible study, he didn't respond. I didn't expect him to. I know he wants me to leave this skeleton in my closet, but I can't. He does not understand the need to explore my feelings. One small part of me intends to go through with the Bible study just because he doesn't want me to. The bigger part of me views this as an outlet where I may be able to talk through some feelings with people who actually care. I need that in my life right now.

The note attached to the reading material says a group is starting in September, and if I am interested I should call right away to reserve my spot. I called the number and said I would be there.

June 25, 1996

There are some days, weeks and even months that come off without a hitch. Given the fact that everything in my life looks perfect on the outside, I fake my way through. The weeks since I last wrote are evidence of that. Busy with our new house, Regi's new job, and lots of company, I didn't have time to dwell on the emptiness inside. Now that the unpacking and rearranging are done, it's difficult not to ponder the inevitable: This month came and went, and I am still not pregnant.

Deciding to tackle the infertility challenge head-on, I made an appointment for my yearly exam with Dr. John Pickens, a gynecologist here in town. I intend to lay everything on the line with him. I've never told any of my doctors about my abortion. But now that I think it might have caused my infertility, I am going to be brave and take a step.

I've thought about how to tell Regi what I am doing but can't determine the best way. Still, he has the right to know what I am about to embark on. I fear facing infertility alone. I long for Regi to talk openly about us having a family one day, but he never does. I am angry that he has abandoned me at this time.

Eventually I will mention my doctor's appointment, but then I'll leave it at that. I want to see if he will even remember to ask me what the doctor says. Sometimes I want to get back at him for making me go through these last months alone. How can he not know I am hurting?

July 4, 1996

Tomorrow is my doctor's appointment and I am scared to death. Not only of what the outcome may be, but also of his reaction when I tell him I had an abortion. He has probably heard the story dozens of times, but tomorrow it will be me in the chair doing the talking.

I have never wanted to risk being placed in that category labeled "damaged goods" because I know how people think of women like me. They assume the worst and cast aspersions upon them. I want people to think of me the same now as they always have, abortion and all.

July 5, 1996

I sat in the waiting room for a good twenty minutes before being called back. After they called my name, I waited in a small area for ten minutes for a nurse to come take my blood. I had plenty of time to make a run for it but didn't dare step outside the sterile area. I waited nervously for someone to appear and get this initial phase over with.

During my extra time, I scanned the equipment around me, noticed labels on the refrigerator, and was impressed by the neatness of each nook and cranny. I liked the place and pictured myself coming back at a later date for an ultrasound or something else having to do with being pregnant.

Directly in front of my chair was a bulletin board filled with pictures of proud parents and siblings showing off the wrinkly newborns this Ob/Gyn office had brought into the world. I quickly scanned the board and claimed one small spot for our baby to be posted.

I calmed my racing heart and fought the urge to believe this bulletin board was a sign. Of what? That I am pregnant? That I would be someday? One thing is certain: I never tire of searching for signs.

When the nurse finished with me and led me into the doctor's private office, I prayed for a non-judgmental doctor. For the first time, I was ready to confess the fears bottled up inside me. I already knew why I couldn't get pregnant; now it was a doctor's turn to confirm it.

After his many questions, I felt my pulse rise and the sweat begin to form. Strength rose up from my toes. I told him my concerns, about the abortion, and how I wanted to pursue a pregnancy. He never flinched but instead reassured me that everything was all right and that he would do his best to get to the bottom of my infertility. He said we may never know the result of my infertility and that it may not stem from the abortion. He told me to stop feeling guilty, accept God's forgiveness, and let it rest! How thankful I am that God sent me to an understanding doctor.

36

There is one hitch. Before any testing can begin on me, Regi must be checked. It is simplest to rule out the man first, but convincing him will be nearly impossible. Lord, give me strength!

July 7, 1996

After I sulked around all day, Regi finally caught on that something was wrong. I didn't give in easily but finally admitted the reason for my dazed depression. My feelings were hurt that he didn't ask how my doctor's appointment went.

It took only a few minutes to lower my defenses and invite Regi into my world, my thoughts. I mustered a smile and opened up. "The doctor was nice, sounded optimistic. He wants to test you, says it probably has nothing to do with the—"

"He wants to do what?"

That was the hard part. I made light of the situation and told him how he had to undergo this simple test. Millions of men have done it. No one would ever know, I assured him. I knew he couldn't refuse; what grounds did he have to resist? I am surprised at how easily he conceded and am encouraged by his willingness.

July 16, 1996

This month's disappointment hit a bit harder than usual. A minor issue between Regi and I hit off two days worth of depression. I attribute it to the underlying evidence–still not pregnant. Maybe it's the surge of extra hormones that permeate my body this time of the month, or maybe it's because I'm keeping track of my feelings. Whatever the reason, I think about having a baby more now than ever before.

July 17, 1996

I just received a phone call from a nurse at Dr. Pickens' office with the results of our first set of infertility tests. As I thought, the problem doesn't lie with Regi, which leaves one incapable person. Today I experienced the first real feelings of helplessness I've had in probably four years.

Until now I've been able to skirt the issue, saying, "We're not really trying," or "It's not His will," or "We're not ready." I broke down in tears after that phone call. Years of wondering and mystery are over, and I ponder where to go from here. Why is God holding out on me? He knows my desires to be a mother! Is He doing this as punishment?

I force my eyes to close and call out to God. He is there waiting, though I don't feel His comfort. I lay my confusion at the altar and weep. I can do nothing else.

July 19, 1996

It has been a few days since I spoke with Mary, the nurse, and received the news of "let the testing begin." I look at my infertility more objectively now. Instead of viewing it with guilt and dread, I think of it with optimism—the first step toward getting pregnant! What a learning process it will be.

I am thankful that God is in this with me and that He orders my life and my steps even before I take them. It is easy to curse my doubt from days before, but I am certain that nothing comes without a cost.

July 22, 1996

Driving to the doctor's office today will be odd. I am alone, my choice, which means I will sit alone in the waiting room and wait alone for the first results. Regi is doing his part, or the most he can do without having to get too involved. I wish he showed more emotion and support, even if it were to say, "Stop." Anything to make me feel like we are in this together.

Today's test will be minimally invasive and painless. It will be a dye test to see what shape my fallopian tubes are in. This will ensure that they are open and working.

Later that day...

As I sat on the examining table, the x-ray technician introduced herself and prepared me for her barrage of questions before the hystereosal pingogram could begin. She asked my name, age, and all that unimportant stuff. Then it hit.

"Have you been pregnant before?"

"Yes."

"Did you carry to full term?"

"No." Good, I thought. She simply assumed I miscarried.

"Miscarriage?" she asked. I contemplated going along with her since the only person that needed to know was the doctor. What if she knows someone, who knows someone who knows me? I haven't gone public with my past; I'm not ready!

"No." My voice crackled, low. "Aborted." I

despise the word and wish I knew her thoughts about me at that second. I could have apologized but didn't.

Yet she went about her job, professionally readying the machines, and didn't say a word. When she did speak her tone of voice was still caring and helpful, as before. Thank You, Lord, for understanding people.

During the test, I watched the screen as Dr. Pickens poked around my insides. He pointed out my uterus and fallopian tubes and found his way through the intricate maze. When I saw my uterus, I could only think of how empty it was. My mind reverted to the baby who lived there for such a short time, and suddenly I felt a bond with this child I never knew. Sadness tugged at my heart.

To Dr. Pickens's satisfaction, the dye spilled out as he hoped and he proclaimed the test a success. Test number two, here I come!

July 23, 1996

Today I wish I had a close friend to call, someone to talk openly and honestly with. The Lord remains my closest friend–He listens and is always available. I can't shake this hesitancy to trust God all the time though. Sitting on the sterile table, awaiting my doctor's response yesterday, I found myself wishing he would find something. If he did, I reasoned, he could fix it and we could get on with an impending pregnancy. If he didn't, I would only be one step closer to owning up to the consequence of a life full of sin. I would never conceive. I don't deserve it.

I can't shake the thoughts about my baby. Writing has helped me heal in the past, and I feel strongly to write to this child. How good it feels to finally acknowledge this child.

Dear Baby,

I saw for the first time a picture of the place God intended human life to begin. Intricately made and delicately placed by His hands.

Before my eyes was a heavenly cradle, a nest, where the perfect temperatures, darkness, and the consistent beating of my heart kept you from getting lonely. I am sorry that I cut you from the only existence you ever knew, away from the hiding place God put you in until you were to be completely formed and ready to be placed in my arms.

For the first time in many years, my arms ached to hold you, to feel your toes and tiny fingers wriggle inside my hand. You are that piece of my life that will be forever missing and that may never completely heal. I've struggled to make sense of my senselessness, though I've not come to grips with any sane reasoning. Perhaps if I had seen even the smallest glimpse of my womb, when you

*filled the empty place with your faint heart-
beat, I wouldn't have made you leave your
home. Now all I have is an empty cavity that
longs to be filled with life again.*

*Knowing you are safe with Jesus is the only
grace that sees me through. So if you see my
tears late at night, or when I am alone,
please don't be sad too. I just wish that I
could see you. But even though I never did,
God did. I am confident that He ushered you
into His presence, to a heaven more
beautiful than I've ever dreamed.*

*I love you, miss you, and look forward to the
day I will finally get to see you.*

July 29, 1996

Today's test, a post-coital, was easy and
painless. Humiliating, but necessary. As I was
called back to a patient waiting room, I left Regi to
flail among the magazines.

Going to the Ob/Gyn's office as a non-pregnant
woman is an emotional thing. I surveyed the
women around me–all largely pregnant. This
waiting room was not suited for women like
myself who desperately want to dress in tents and
have swollen feet. I overheard two women talking
about their impending ultrasounds, and how
they've consumed enough water to float. Today's
test would allow them to paint the nursery blue or
pink. I watched another woman and her husband
as they nervously fingered the VHS tape that

would capture their first glimpse of their child.

I handled everything pretty well until yet another pregnant woman walked in, her breathing in sync with her husband's counts. Active labor, no doubt. I prayed to be called out of this torture chamber soon. As tears welled up, my name was called and I was rescued.

After the test, I waited for a few minutes until the results were ready. Once again, he found nothing wrong and remarked that this is a good sign. We will get to the bottom of this, he assured me. How I wish he were right.

August 10, 1996

With the onset of cramps, another month of not being pregnant comes. It happens uneventfully, and I pray for strength to get through the day.

My prayer time this morning centers on finding happiness in fluctuating circumstances. I am so guilty of basing my security on things like what the weather is like. Ridiculous! My morning walk with the dog confirms just that.

I beat the day's high humidity factor by starting out early. An abnormally cool August breeze brushes my body as I step out the front door and see blue skies as far as my eye travels. A few white billows of clouds interrupt the blue masterpiece but complement the Artist's work. What a glorious day. Immediately my mind wanders to thoughts such as, "I could do so much today...write a book, start a business, and fill the house with the scent of freshly baked cookies." My walk is a bit peppier today and I race to keep up with the dog. But if the brilliant blue sky determines my happiness, what about the times when it rains?

At this point in my life, the rain has taken on different forms. A new job, a new home, the desire to have a baby, the need for friends–all circumstances that are able to change in a moment's time.

The baby issue is all-consuming. I am beginning to understand the lessons God is teaching me. First of all, if my future happiness rests on conceiving and raising a child, then I may never be blessed with one. Why? Because my ultimate happiness must be in Jesus. I wade into dangerous waters when my focus shifts from Him.

The hope of it all, however, is that the infertility issue constantly brings me closer to the Lord. I do get sad, mostly at this time of month, and long for a child. There are moments when I don't know how I will hide the tears, but I do. If I went around crying all day, unable to look at a baby or a pregnant woman, I would not have peace or faith. Yet the very fact that I can get through each day resting on Him signifies that I have peace. Thanks to God.

The Lord is my light and hope. He knows my heart, my past and my future, and He still loves me. I cannot fathom such an unconditional love. I am grateful that I can depend on Him, not only as my Savior and Forgiver, but also as my Friend.

August 12, 1996

The phone rings. It is a friend who is dealing with a rough second pregnancy. She speaks of her mixed joy in taking care of one baby and preparing for another. I cannot relate to her roller coaster ride but identify with her stress.

I try to be a friend and listen to what is going on with her. This second pregnancy is a surprise and she feels she isn't ready for another baby yet. How I wish I were in her shoes. I would love to bring her into my world of disappointment, but I don't think she could understand. I have shared our inability to conceive with her and her husband, but they are careful not to probe too deep. If I could tell her, and others like her, my innermost thoughts, maybe she could begin to feel what it's like to live in such a canyon of darkness. What I would give for just one day of her morning sickness...

August 20, 1996

Facing the guilt of my abortion, struggling with the fear of infertility, the place I am today–all coincide with my devotions, that is, poverty of spirit, an absence of self-assurance, self-reliance and pride. It is the deepest form of repentance. It is turning from my independence to total dependence on God. It is brokenness. "I am to welcome anything that will break me, that will bend my knees and bring me to utter destitution before God." (Kay Arthur, *Lord, Only You Can Change Me*).

The understanding comes like a streak of lightning across the bruised sky. The Lord is tired of my self-reliance and independence. I am not totally broken before Him, nor am I destitute for Him. As usual, He hits me where it's most personal, and where I can do nothing but cling to Him. That is the place I am today.

46

> *I love the Lord, for he heard my voice; he heard my cry for mercy. Because he turned his ear to me, I will call on him as long as I live. The cords of death entangled me, the anguish of the grave came upon me; I was overcome by trouble and sorrow. Then I called on the name of the Lord: "O Lord, save me!" The Lord is gracious and righteous; our God is full of compassion. The Lord protects the simplehearted; when I was in great need, he saved me. Be at rest once more, O my soul, for the Lord has been good to you. For you, O Lord, have delivered my soul from death, my eyes from tears, my feet from stumbling, that I may walk before the Lord in the land of the living. I believed;*

therefore I said, "I am greatly afflicted." And in my dismay I said, "All men are liars." How can I repay the Lord for all his goodness to me?

—Psalm 116:1-12, NIV

August 23, 1996

Lord, with every approaching day and situation, I find I need You more. Before I prepare to turn even this next corner of my life, I pray my dependency upon You grows.

I am back from a much-needed vacation only to be reminded that my womb still remains barren. My spirit is down, maybe from the quiet of the house and the longing in my soul.

I am not a quitter. I am more than a conqueror! The waiting has become an eternity and causes me to doubt. I ask forgiveness one more time. The journey is hard, but the reward will be sweet.

August 24, 1996

Today rolls in like a lion. The knowledge that something is wrong with me, possibly a greater complication than we can imagine, is too much for me to handle. I know the Lord has a plan for my life, but am I living in the midst of it? Please, God, no! I want to be healed and skip whatever else I need to learn.

47

I resist the urge to raise my fist toward heaven and curse the reason for my existence. I wish I could turn back the hands of time and do things right this time. I am a failure who has managed to hurt everyone I know.

The tears are heavier today than usual, more abundant too. If there's ever been a time when I need to feel the promises of God lift me up, it's today. Right now. I need His strength. He has not called me to failure or sadness, but to complete life in Him. I feel every bit of my humanity, weak and insecure. I am not afraid to say I need Him once again, or to say I've failed in my human attempt to be strong and have faith. I am scared and I pray for the power to cling to His Word and allow His healing power to cleanse me.

August 25, 1996

I arrived at church late enough to miss the idle chatter but not late enough to go unnoticed. I can't answer one more "How are you" with a blatant lie of "Just fine." I don't want to see one more cute little girl dressed in pink tights and red bows. I see a woman slant her head, crinkle her eyebrows and whisper words to her friend. I automatically assume someone has told them about my problem and they want to know more, maybe even pray for me.

I do not allow my lips to speak unless spoken to.

My arms stay by my side in rebellion, and I wish I had just stayed home. But I know the best place for me to be tonight is in church even though I have forced myself. I pray with my eyes open because it is easier to fight the tears this way. They don't find their way down.

The worship service begins and the songs move me. I feel better already. I still keep to myself since the irritation factor is high. For a moment, I feel the burden lift from my shoulders as I allow God's Spirit to take its place in my heart.

September 3, 1996

49

The phone rings and interrupts my silence. It is Dr. Pickens. When I hear his voice, it signals that something is wrong. Why else would he call personally?

In his optimistic doctor's voice, he says I have nothing to worry about. All that will be required is outpatient surgery–easy stuff. He must say that to all his patients. What else would he say, "It's looks bad. You'll never be able to conceive"?

He says the hystereosalpingogram wasn't a success after all. When he attempted to inject dye through my fallopian tubes, it looked as if it spilled out, the way it should have. But upon a closer look he noticed it actually pooled up, not spilling out anywhere. This was proof that something was blocking them. His next procedure would be a laparoscopy in about a week and a half to survey the extent of the damage and see if it can be corrected.

It hits like a freight train, and I know that whatever is there is an artifact from everything I've ever done wrong in my life–the abortion, the sin, the immorality. As if I don't have enough stale leftovers in my life! Atonement is here.

September 10, 1996

Part of me feels relief that I have something to go on now–a reason to stop wondering every month why I'm not pregnant, or a reason to hope. The other part of me grapples with an undeniable fear, a nausea that tickles my stomach every evening when I lie awake in bed. God does not give me this spirit of fear, yet I am paralyzed by it.

If it weren't for the Lord, I would be alone tonight. Regi sleeps peacefully, dreaming of tomorrow, while I stare at the ceiling in hopes of seeing His faint handwriting. Nothing. Regi doesn't ask how I am and still shows no emotion about the whole process. I certainly can't wake him up and say I want to talk. If I never pursued why we aren't able to get pregnant, he would never question it. I long for him to be more interested!

Maybe he doesn't ask because he's afraid of what I'll tell him, afraid of knowing everything there is. I'm ashamed that I may not be able to give him children and wonder if he resents me. I wish I had told him in the beginning, but I didn't think it mattered. I was wrong. If I could tell him how I feel, I would say that I'm nervous about Monday and fearful of the consequences. If the outcome is worse than expected, how will he feel? Cheated? Lied to? I worry about what is going through his head, if anything, but defer from probing. He may have anger lodged there, and I don't think I can deal with his anger on top of mine. I only hope he has some emotion hiding behind his eyes.

My mom will be coming in tomorrow to help out if anything is needed. She wants to be with me during this time, as only a mom can be. I don't know how I'll feel after the surgery, and she'll be around to lend an extra hand if needed. I wonder how she is dealing with this impending infertility and the thoughts that she may never be a grandmother. I wish I could share my deepest thoughts with her, but I'm too scared. I still cannot face my past.

Speaking of my past, my post-abortion Bible study group starts the day of my surgery, and I will not be able to go. I won't miss anything except introductions and an overview. God's timing is so perfect, and I am happy to finally start the Bible study. The fact that I haven't dealt with my abortion is clear since I'm convinced that everything I am experiencing is because of it. I pray the upcoming weeks shed some light into my darkness.

September 16, 1996

This is it! The day of my outpatient surgery. Today I will gain a greater insight into what is going on inside this body.

It has become quite obvious that I deal with stress differently from anyone around me, especially my husband. Yesterday in church, I was robbed of joy because of my stress. We ended up in a heated discussion about something that was not even the cause of my emotional state, and I received nothing out of the sermon. Until yesterday, my stress and worry over this laparoscopy were tucked deep inside my hip pocket. Not so anymore! I emptied those pockets and lets words I didn't even mean fly.

For weeks now, I have been anxious, nervous, lonely and unsure. I wish I knew someone who has been through infertility who could help me understand my feelings. Isn't there someone who can validate my mixed bag of emotions? I must know that I haven't lost it mentally! As nice as it is to have a "trying to understand to the best of his ability husband" and a "mom who doesn't know everything but wants to help," they cannot fully comprehend my heart and mind. Their efforts to help comfort me a bit, and I am thankful for them, but I am just plain scared of the next step.

Many friends called and prayed with me about this operation. One said she had been thinking about me and felt led to call me. Even before I told her what I would be facing today, she gave me some words of wisdom that I believe were truly from God. "Fear not," she told me, "you have won." Her prayers were right in line with three other people who prayed for me at church last night also. They said things like, "God, give her all the children she desires, for we know she will give them back to You. You know the miracle she needs, and she'll give You the glory." They must be reading from the same Book! God is so good.

I have tried, however, not to talk about the surgery with too many people. I still cannot fully disclose everything with them, thus I tread lightly. What I really want someone to say to me is, "This is not happening because of your past sin. God has forgiven you. He has washed you from within." Only the Lord knows the weight I carry and why I can't seem to give it all to Him. God is with me, and I feel Him as I prepare to leave for the hospital.

At the surgery center, I changed into my hospital cap and gown and was placed in a holding tank where they would prep me before taking me into the operating room. The last time I was in a place like this was when I had the abortion. Today it is just as sterile as then, but the fear is not as intense.

I tried to relax, but my heart was beating too fast. It occurred to me that my whole life had led up to that moment in time. I never dreamed I would be there, facing these difficulties, dealing with these demons. I repeated Psalm 103 to myself, determined to praise Him for all my benefits. As I was wheeled back, I asked God to send His angels ahead and to light the way. I asked Him to be with Dr. Pickens and to give him wisdom in whatever decision he would have to make. I also prayed that He would prepare me for whatever lies ahead, and that I will continue to trust His perfect timing for my whole life.

Thank you, Lord, for your guidance, Your support and Your grace that covers me. You are my eternal hope, all I'll ever need.

54

September 18, 1996

It has been two days since that rainy drive to the hospital. On our way, we saw the most beautiful rainbow illuminating the sky. It stretched across the sky in splendor. It looked as if it started on top of the hospital and reached to join hands with the area where I live. I took it as a confirmation that everything was going to be okay.

I remember trying to bring myself back from the drug-induced sleep after the surgery. I could hear soft voices trying to arouse me, but my eyes wouldn't open. I desperately wanted to wake up and find out what happened.

When I was fully awake, my husband and mother came immediately to my side with strained smiles. Something wasn't right. They talked about everything but the outcome. I looked great. How did I feel? They laughed at all the blankets covering me. I went along with their chatter as long as I could, thinking only of one thing. I asked when Dr. Pickens would be back to talk to me, and they said he had already spoken to them. I was pumped up on drugs, but I knew something wasn't right.

No one was talking, and it made me mad. Besides, why were they standing so far away and not acting like I was lying in a hospital bed hooked up to some crazy monitor? Their feeling went beyond that of concern for my health and comfort. It was more of a consolation for something they had yet to say.

When Regi said, "He couldn't unblock your tubes," I thought he was playing a lousy joke. The moment was awkward. Was I supposed to cry? Or should I act like it didn't bother me? I felt myself shrink to nothing. He kept on, saying there were too many adhesions and that it was too risky to do anything beyond cleaning up some of the scar tissue. Our next option, and best chance, would be in vitro fertilization.

With those words, I started to cry. My mother started to cry. They offered support that couldn't begin to console my heavy heart. The doctor may as well have said I would never have children because IVF was as out of reach as anything that moment. There was no way we could afford the thousands of dollars that IVF would cost, and the complications and failure rate made my heart callous. It wasn't even a remote possibility.

During the rest of my recovery time at the hospital I tried to be happy. Another cover-up. When the doctor called to check up on me, my voice quivered, something that became a habit over the next few days. He said the adhesions could be attributed to any number of factors; there was no way of ever knowing. My uterus and ovaries were fine and he would see me the next day to take out a stitch in my naval. "Don't worry, there's still hope."

56

From the moment I returned home, I concentrated on getting well. Nothing else. The medication made me very sick. I was nauseous and passed out repeatedly. Only I knew that tears were slowly building up in the caverns of my heart, ready to spew forth at any second.

Regi and Mom took great care of my physical needs, but only I could work on the emotional ones. Every time the phone rang, I heard my mom or Regi quietly repeat the death sentence that had already been handed down.

That night, my mom went to her room, and Regi settled me into bed. Not an easy process due to the soreness. He turned the light off and went into the bathroom to prepare for bed.

I was alone for the first time. I felt a storm brewing on the inside, and I could not control the tears. I did not want Regi to see me cry or see my weakness. This was my entire fault, rooted in layers of past sin, and I would deal with the issues, not him or anyone else. I could not bring them into my world of pain because they didn't deserve it.

No matter what I did, my pillow became soaked, and I couldn't hide the pain. Like a loving husband, Regi did what he could, the best he knew how. He consoled me, held me and reaffirmed me. Nothing more could be done to ease my pain for the moment. The torment I felt at that moment was the kind of pain I would have to get used to. It superseded any leftover pain from the operation I had just come through.

September 19, 1996

The house is so quiet today it is almost deafening. The kitchen is void of cabinets closing, silverware rattling or coffee perking by someone other than myself. Mom left last night, and Regi has plans to leave early this morning for a long awaited golf outing. I did not sleep well last evening, and the effects of little sleep put my emotions on the vulnerable side. Lying here in bed, I start preparing myself for the first day alone. I don't want to be here with my thoughts, my depression or my useless body. Once again, I know if I cry I'll never stop.

If Regi sees me like this, he'll never leave me alone. Yet I know he needs to get out of the house for a day of golf with his friends. The knock on the bedroom door interrupts my thoughts, and I sense he will be gone in a few minutes. The seconds are racing.

The only thing I know to do is call my mother. If I am at least on the phone when Regi leaves, the silence won't be so hard to deal with. I realize that our home will be quiet like this for many years to come.

I haven't prayed about my new sentence since it was handed down to me. I find a bit of solace in writing, but none in God. I feel betrayed and don't want to cry out to Him any longer. If I keep God at arm's length, maybe I won't say things I don't mean.

I dial the phone and hear my mom's voice all the way from Dallas. When she hears the tremble in my voice, she becomes upset. I tell her that I just want to be talking to someone when Regi leaves so I can postpone the silence. She knows she should have stayed longer and decides to come back. It was too soon to leave me, she concludes, although I don't admit she is right. She will be here by this evening.

Regi offered to stay home when he saw how upset I was, but I wouldn't allow it. This was his day and he deserved it. I know he felt horrible leaving me in such a ridiculous state, so he did what he could. He called one of my girlfriends and had her check up on me by showing up unexpectedly.

When my mom arrived, relief swept over me. This meant I could put off being alone for a few more days. Though I've lived with the fear of infertility for so long, speculation is far different from confirmation. I thought I could get around it by not knowing what the true problem was. Had I known knowledge would hurt so much, I may never have sought the answer. I feel like a failure first to God, then to my husband and family, then to myself. It is the worst feeling I've ever known.

September 22, 1996

We spent last night with friends, and it felt good to get out of the house. I've stayed cooped up too long. No one asked how I was feeling until the end of the evening. I wondered if they would ask, and of course, how I would respond. As much as I didn't want to go over all the details, it was crazy acting like nothing had happened.

A few times during dinner I noticed stares from a few people–that "what a gal," candy-coated look. I felt like I was living the inside of a disgusting Hallmark card. Before the night was over, someone asked if we had looked into adoption. Wrong question! No, we hadn't discussed adoption, but thank you anyway for your simple resolution to my grand problem. It's not about adoption. It's about me and the fact that I will never have children.

September 23, 1996

I quietly slipped into the Bible study, unaware of what to expect. Would the people be friendly or hard to get to know? Camping out in left field or pretty normal? The leader of the group called me earlier this week, so at least I know her a little bit and don't feel like such an outsider.

The group consists of three women plus the instructor, all whom have had abortions. We are all a bit tentative at first but warm up soon and make conversation about husbands, children and ourselves. What strikes me as odd is that we are all so normal! Women who become mothers, have important careers and are upstanding Christians sometimes have abortions in their past–what a novel thought. It makes me think that even my own friends whom I would never suspect could be in the same predicament I'm in–afraid to talk about their past for fear that no one will accept them or understand.

We spent the evening going over our outline and discussing what we hoped to gain from the Bible study. The topics are pretty heavy, and the study book will bring out issues I've not thought about in ten years.

September 24, 1996

Today marked one week since the surgery and ill-fated news. I've confessed my sin of blaming God and distancing myself from Him when I needed Him the most. When I went to church Sunday night, I cried the moment worship started. God met me there, even though I had turned my back on Him the days before. Until that moment, I was afraid to pray because that meant I had to face my situation. This is clearly not the time to start questioning His will. I continue to fight the fear that this is my punishment and am awaiting a sign from Him to contradict those feelings.

I serve a God of love, not of punishment and condemnation. I serve a God of forgiveness, not a God who remembers my sin. His mercy gently reaffirms my darkened spirit.

September 25, 1996

Almost overnight, I feel as though I have begun lowering my defenses and allowing God His rightful place into my life again. I never knew I was so stubborn until now. My heart feels full, yet empty at the same time. I think of the wonderful sacrifice this will be if He decides to heal me and use my testimony somehow. Encouragement comes from the words, "God gives me nothing I cannot handle." That is one statement I am determined to put to the test!

For now, I pray this proclamation over my life: Lord, I resign myself to You. Use me according to Your plan, and let me be a vessel for Your grace. Grant my body and mind healing, according to Your loving kindness, and grant me the desires of my heart. Draw me closer to You, not just for this season, but for eternity.

September 26, 1996

I sat on the patio today and felt the wind lift my hair as if to prepare my body for flight. I wish it were so easy! It is the silence that overtakes me again as I am ready to call it a day. The half-moon is prepared to take over when the sun leaves its spot for the night. What exactly does another day mean for me? Staying busy doing nothing important? This will only send me deeper into the chasm I've created for myself. It is depressing on breezy nights when no one is home.

September 27, 1996

I've decided to find my favorite scriptures that

pertain to this time in my life and dwell on them daily. It will help most during the times I doubt or fear God's provision for me.

> *Praise the Lord, O my soul, and forget not all his benefits—who forgives all your sins and heals all your diseases, who redeems your life from the pit and crowns you with love and compassion, who satisfies your desires with good things so that your youth is renewed like the eagle's.*
>
> —Psalm 103:2-5, NIV

> *Worship the Lord your God, and his blessing will be on your food and water. I will take away sickness from among you, and none will miscarry or be barren in your land. I will give you a full life span.*
>
> —Exodus 23:25-26, NIV

> *Delight yourself in the Lord and he will give you the desires of your heart.*
>
> *Commit your way to the Lord; trust in him and he will do this.*   —Psalm 37:4-5, NIV

God's Word remains the direction for every aspect of my life. As usual, when the chips have fallen, the need to drink from His well intensifies. Oh that I would daily have an intense need for Him, even when the battles are few.

September 30, 1996

Today as I sat on the porch listening to the rain ping softly on the roof, a hummingbird revisited the nectar that hung from a tiny birdfeeder. With incredible zeal, he returns again, eating as much as half his weight. He flutters next to the feeder, making quick jolts with his neck to get as close as he can to sip the sweetness waiting for him. He will return until the nectar is gone, of that I can be sure.

As I sat mesmerized by the hummingbird's efforts, the phone rang and a lawn company made an appointment to come and treat my lawn so that springtime would find the grass green and lush. "Pre-emergent," he called it, which simply means he would fertilize it to prevent the weeds from taking over. "The groundwork for a beautiful lawn," he tells me.

As silly as it sounds, the analogies are close to my relationship with God. His Word is there for me every moment of the day and waits for me to spend time soaking up its promises. It is sweet to my needful body. Unlike the hummingbird, I'm not zealous, as if my life depended on it. Instead, something always hinders me from feeding on His Word, such as messy dishes, a telephone call or even church activities. I am like my dog whenever he catches sight of the hummingbird. Immediately his attention is diverted from whatever he is doing and he gives chase. The simple things of life too easily distract me.

Like that green lawn I desire, help me to cultivate an intimate relationship with You, Lord, so that I will be fruitful, not bearing bad seed and weeds!

October 2, 1996

I had my post-op check-up with Dr. Pickens today. I realized something as I was getting ready to go to his office. I was due to start my cycle a few days ago, and it never even occurred to me. In some ways it's a relief to know I won't be holding my breath month after month now, waiting for the signs of pregnancy. It is bittersweet.

Once again I entered his office only to be faced with a couple of big-bellied women in what looked to be their third trimester of pregnancy. I wished they wouldn't complain about their swollen feet and aching backs. I would change places with them in a second. I stuck my head in a magazine and tried to drown out their talk.

I was doing well until the ride home from Dr. Pickens' office. How silly I felt when I stopped at a red light that happened to be in front of a maternity store. Six pregnant mannequins stood in the window, all wearing the latest winter maternity fashions. For every insane reason I could think of, I began to cry. I shed tears over fake pregnant people!

I believe that telling a woman she can't conceive is equal to telling her she has no significance. Havoc continues to battle in my mind that I am worthless to my husband and myself.

October 3, 1996

I am alone today. This incredible feeling of emptiness takes up where my strength fails. Again the tears race down my face. The first one is easy to fight, but the second and third ones are determined to prevail. I am tired of feeling this way and tired of being utterly helpless.

It is painful to cry, and I want to scream away the pain. I don't know what else to do because I thought that once I relinquished my problem to God, I could handle the infertility with ease. Am I never supposed to spend another minute alone? Should I hide my feelings, even far from my own reach?

When I reached for my Bible, it felt heavy. It opened to Hosea–wonderful, a book I know nothing about. Verse one is meaningless, as is verse two, and on and on, until chapter 2 verse 14. Miraculously, God is faithful to speak to me. Not by proxy or a casual thought, but by His written Word. I'd like to think that if Hosea chapter 2 were a letter to me, it would go something like this.

Dear Kim,

"Therefore I am now going to allure her; I will lead her into the desert and speak tenderly to her. There I will give her back her vineyards, and will make the Valley of Achor a door of hope. There she will sing as in the days of her youth, as in the day she came up out of Egypt."

I would respond:

Dear God,

I am in the desert, awaiting a sign from You. My life has never felt so empty, so seared from guilt and shame, condemned from sin. The only thing that can allure me is Your tenderness, Your voice speaking softly and calmly to my pain.

I pray for You to restore my shattered dreams lost to a lifetime of selfishness. Rebuild my castles that once were beautiful with Your favor. Please change this door of trouble to a door of hope, and don't allow it to open more strife upon my tear-soaked life. Let me sing with the angels, a song of my youth; a song of innocence, a song of praise to You.

God would then respond:

Dear Kim,

"I will betroth you to me forever; I will betroth you in righteousness and justice, in love and compassion. I will betroth you in faithfulness, and you will acknowledge the Lord. 21 "In that day I will respond," declares the Lord - "I will respond to the skies, and they will respond to the earth; and the earth will respond to the grain, the new wine and oil, and they will respond to Jezreel. I will plant her for myself in the land; I will show my love to the one I called 'Not my loved one.' I will say to those called 'Not my people,' 'You are my people'; and they will say, 'You are my God.' "

I love you.

68

Dear God,

Thank You for loving me, a sinner who has no one else to turn to. You've opened Your door of hope upon my hopelessness and rebirthed in me a new beginning. Your hope brings dryness to my sobbing eyes and peace to my troubled heart. In you I have a refuge, a hiding place, protection from further torment. I long to carry these promises with me always. Please write them on my heart forever.

I love you!

October 6, 1996

This morning I read from Jeremiah 32 and 33. I have always loved 32:17, "...nothing is too difficult for you," but have usually prayed that for someone else and believed it as their miracle. Now I believe it for me. How I pray for faith, the courage to allow it to grow and increase according to His plan. God says that nothing is too difficult for Him, and I stand on that same promise He gave Jeremiah. I ask Him to assure me. Restore me. Fill my emptiness with His fullness. Replace my mourning with joy.

As I continued in Jeremiah, He gave me the verse from 33:6, "Nevertheless, I will bring health and healing to it; I will heal my people and will let them enjoy abundant peace and security." NIV

69

As I stood at the altar yesterday in church, I felt myself beginning to receive His healing, His miracle. I asked that my life would be a testimony of His grace and goodness. I am not ashamed! At His feet, I left the remnants of my broken life and decided to begin trusting His timing, His ways.

I don't know what to expect now. Will I have moments of sadness still? If I do, does that mean I've not completely given the feelings of insignificance to Him? I must allow the Holy Spirit to be my comforter; I don't want to leave His presence unchanged.

There may still be times I feel He isn't with me, when the emptiness overtakes the joy. It is these times when I've looked around and felt banished by the crowd that I realize just what God means to me. He is my Friend, my truest Friend, and it has come down to He and I. Even if no one ever understands, it will be okay. If no one ever feels my pain, it will be just fine. I will always have the Lord on my side.

October 14, 1996

This past week I was challenged by the question, How far will I go for a successful pregnancy? In talking to some close friends, I was forced to examine the question further. What is this pursuit all about? Is it an obsession with wanting a baby, the need to be needed? Or is it the pursuit of a family, the desire to offer a loving environment to children earmarked as "unwanted." I dare say this desire is for the latter, because it is lasting, unlike the baby stage, which is fleeting. If that is truly the case, my field of opportunity is instantly expanded. I contemplate my next move, planning carefully for the intended results.

My heart is capable of loving anyone, that I know. It would be a lie to say I don't dream of bearing my own children, of seeing a piece of Regi and me passed on. I want to see my eyes and his smile in another human being. Does that mean that if I never conceive, we won't be able to pass a piece of ourselves on? That someone, somewhere, couldn't come to know me as "Mom" is overwhelming and ludicrous. I will consider everything, for God's intention for my life may not be clear at the present, but it is there for me to seek.

How far will I go to have a family? I don't know. Am I willing to attempt that distance? Yes.

October 22, 1996

The past two weeks have been pretty good ones. I've not thought much about anything, just stayed busy and focused on the Lord's will for me. Will I ever know it?

I received advice this weekend contrary to any I've yet to hear. This time it was from a loving family member. When speaking about my "impending barrenness," she actually said it was a blessing. A blessing? Given the state of society (I've heard this one before), why would I want to bring a child into this world? I should take my current health status as a sign from God that children are not part of His plan for me.

The words came down like a knife on a chopping block. Cut and dry. I, being the meek and mild introvert, soaked it in, as if I agreed. However, there is not a bone in my body that believes God does not intend for me to be a mother. Why do some women regret their years of motherhood, of bandaging scraped knees and baking chocolate chip cookies? In blatant honesty, maybe she feels she never should have had children. Why then does everyone else proclaim that some of their richest blessings in life come from their children?

October 29, 1996

I am reading about Paul this morning, starting with Philippians 1. The words pierce my heart with a new sensitivity and understanding. Instead of being words on a page, it is as though Paul himself is reading aloud to me from his jail cell as he writes the letter. I reread it to gain the full impact of each word.

Paul viewed his imprisonment as a way to advance the gospel–imagine that! Even in chains he found a way to be happy in the Lord. The situation isn't what he planned or expected, but he is there for the ultimate defense of God's Word.

"...I will continue to rejoice...for I know what has happened to me will turn out for my deliverance...for me to live is Christ and to die is gain." Did Paul realize that his ancient words would speak volumes to me in 1996? The inspiration is found through his indifferent attitude toward God's will upon his life. Nothing else matters, except that Jesus Christ is glorified and preached. He doesn't voice concern over whether his family is taken care of. That the business he left is thriving or, in my case, that I may not be able to bear children. All that matters is living for Christ, for by dying, we still gain!

As Paul continues on about Christ, he portrays his attitude concisely: "...taking the very nature of a servant...he humbled himself and became obedient even to death...." Jesus was humble, obedient and subservient to His Father's will for His life. He never questioned. Never doubted. He left a throne in heaven for a life on earth. In His greatness, He became a sacrifice for me.

Why do I stumble, hesitate, even doubt His love for me? I question His grace each time I curse the depression and loneliness I'm in. When I say "Why?" I deny that I trust Him. I want to be like Paul, bold in my faith, ready to do anything for the sake of His gospel. Whatever God's will is for my life, I pray I will learn to live in its knowledge without remorse or hesitation.

> *Do not be anxious about anything, but in everything, by prayer and petition, with thanksgiving, present your requests to God.*
>
> **—Philippians 4:6, NIV**

October 31, 1996

Today I am more knowledgeable on the process of IVF than ever before. Not only did I buy my first book on the subject and read it halfway already, I am going to have lunch with a new friend who has been through one unsuccessful round of IVF.

I listen to Kathy and ask a ton of questions. I hear the pain in her voice as she tells me how her eggs were extracted, fertilized and then placed into her uterus. Days of bed rest and wondering followed, only to find out that the eggs didn't take. It doesn't take long for me to realize that IVF may not be for us. For one, I don't see how we could afford it. Besides, it comes with no guarantees and no absolutes.

I want to cry for Kathy. I want to cry for me. I want to weep for the person who just found out their attempt to create a child was unsuccessful. Noting the low percentages of IVF heightens my dependence on God. I rest in the promise He gave in Hosea 2: "I will give her vineyards...and the Valley of Achor for a door of hope."

On the way home from lunch, I find peace in crossing IVF off my list of possibilities. Relief! I am not against this method and pray that one day we can take that route. Surprisingly I don't feel sad. The fact that God answered me revitalizes my faith. Just to know He hasn't forgotten about me gives me the will to trudge forward. He has something waiting for me, and one day I will receive it.

November 12, 1996

With my face made up and my clothes pressed, I am off to my first baby shower since finding out about my infertility. I am leaving my emotions at home in order to enjoy the evening with friends in celebration for this new life. I can do it!

Last Sunday night at church a girl sat behind me with an infant. Immediately I smiled at her, an automatic response for her wonderful blessing. I didn't second guess her presence or ponder the fact that a baby was just behind me. Another normal occurrence, right? Wrong! When the baby cried for its next feeding, the mother gave him a bottle as expected. My eyes welled up the minute I heard him sucking. I tried not to let the people on each side of me notice. I debated getting up from my chair and leaving to avoid creating a small scene. About that time, the woman took the child out of the service, much to my relief.

By now I am accustomed to this water faucet of emotions that turn on and off for no major reason. Every time I feel like I am back to normal, they are triggered by the smallest whimper of a baby or the casual glance of someone I know. I long for people to treat me normally and not with pitiful eyes for what is wrong with me. I want people to ask me how I am doing instead of avoiding the topic of children altogether. I don't want them to shove their children in my face in an effort to fill the void, but I do want people to stop saying what a blessing it is not to have children! When I hear comments like that, I want to snatch their children from their lives, all the memories, fun and kisses, and let them see how wonderful it is without them. If they could live in my shoes for just one day and feel the pain that gnaws at me! God, grant people just a little bit of wisdom. No, grant them common sense! So, with baggage in tow, I enter the festivities.

As I walk into the gathering, people greet me as usual and I make my way to my friends. Okay so far. I pass the gifts around as if I am interested and talk about things other than babies. The expectant mother says her tearful thank-yous and pats her stomach with pride. I feel okay but decide to skip the refreshments and make my way home after an hour or so.

On my way to the car, I fumble with the keys. I can't figure out which one is which because my eyes are pouring tears. Who was I fooling when I said I could do this? The nine-mile drive home takes forever, and I wish I had the guts to keep driving as far away from my life, my home and my pain as I could possibly get. I never thought life would be like this.

When I get home, Regi immediately asks what is wrong. I can't hide my puffy eyes and red face from him. I escape to our bedroom and lock myself in. If Regi can't figure out what is wrong with me, he doesn't deserve an explanation. It doesn't take a genius to see that I am hurting.

November 15, 1996

I learn more and more everyday in the midst of my greatest trials. God is all I need and all that matters to me. It is not about other people, meeting their expectations or not, what becomes of me, or who I become. It is about my relationship with my Lord and Savior! I cannot fathom how He weathers all these storms with me, even sticking with me through the depression and mood swings. No one is this faithful and true.

77

November 30, 1996

Thanksgiving meets me amidst a cornucopia of emotions. Highs and lows, good and bad. They all correlate with who I am and who I've become.

I am thankful for much and continually remind myself of such. My happiness is not based on the fact that I don't have a child to call my own. It is easy to admit this revelation when my spirits are high. It is when they fluctuate that I have to remind myself of this. Who knows, if life were an even-keeled boat ride, it might get a little boring!

Coming away from this Thanksgiving, our sixth since being married, life gently takes on a new perspective as we drive home. We place great emphasis on being with family during the holidays. In the process we lose our sanity and experience incredible bouts of stress. I long for my family to be together, consisting of my husband, myself and, one day, our own children. I want to make our own traditions, in our own home. I know it will happen eventually.

We drive through the haze of the early morning, the rain of the afternoon and the stillness of the twilight. For a short weekend we escaped all that clouds our minds, but we still return to where we left it. Ahead of us lie decisions we've yet to agree on and a future that holds many promises. I am happy to return to my life as I know it, even with its rough terrain. No matter the circumstances, I wouldn't trade my life, my husband, my faith for anything.

Maybe it takes a holiday like Thanksgiving for me to truly give thanks for the blessings I receive daily.

December 10, 1996

The Bible study I've been involved in is officially over. Thirteen weeks have flown by, and much has happened since beginning this study. God's timing was perfect, as I started this intense healing right as I found out about the infertility. You'd have a hard time telling me the two don't go hand in hand.

I remember skimming through my reading material and thinking that none of it pertained to me. How wrong I was! I now know that much of who I am today is because of all that happened to me in the past. It is wonderful to see myself for who I really am, not for someone everyone else wants me to be. God loves me for me, all of me, and will use the real me if I allow Him. He certainly won't use someone who is puffed up and wearing the world's facade.

Now that the abortion issue has finally been dealt with, I am ready to move on to whatever the Lord has for my life now. I pray I take all I've learned into this darkened world so that others will see their light of hope and healing. I continue to pray for the perfect timing of when God will use my testimony. Though I have so much more to learn, I want desperate women like myself to gain final acceptance and forgiveness from the Lord for the scar of abortion.

79

God has a plan for my life, and I don't want to stop pressing into Him until I uncover it. I am available to Him, ready for the next step. Somehow, through the pains and questions my entire life has yielded, I feel as though I am about to burst from the joy I feel today. That joy comes from the knowledge that no matter where my life leads, I am safe with God's guiding hand.

January 13, 1997

The New Year is upon us and leaves me reeling with amazement at the velocity with which it came. I have neglected my journal writing, perhaps out of exasperation, pity or just plain boredom. But like an old friend, the blank pages invite me in once again and I get lost among the words.

In many ways, I am grateful that 1996 is behind me. This is a time for new beginnings, a time to stop contemplating the old and prepare for the good days ahead.

I vow that this year I will immerse myself in God's presence. My dependency has come full circle. I tried dealing with my pain without Him and failed. Thankfully I know that He has already accepted me back! He never changed, but I sure did. He remains an anchor in my ever-changing life, a constant I constantly count on!

January 31, 1997

This past week I found out that two friends are pregnant. One was Kathy, the friend who spoke to me about her first round of in vitro fertilization. Her second attempt at IVF proved successful. I am honestly excited for her and know God answered many prayers. I prayed for her during this second round and somehow feel overwhelmed at the prospect that my prayer has been answered.

Then I found out that another friend who has been trying for two years just discovered she is pregnant. Even though we've lost touch over the miles, I silently hoped she would call and share her good news. I need to know that God still answers prayers! I find encouragement in their joy.

I would be dishonest if I said I haven't felt a tinge of pain amidst all the happiness. Now I don't know anyone who is faced with infertility, and it is a lonely feeling. The pain still reverberates from time to time, but not as plaguing as before. There were even times this week, around friends, when I questioned if I was cut out for motherhood! The whining, dirty diapers, throw-up and threats grew old quickly. For once I was glad to come home to the quiet and my dog.

I continue to rely on God to heal me. I cling to Scripture verses such as 2 Kings 5:20 and Psalm 103:3-5. I feel no strong urge to pursue IVF or adoption and continue to trust the Lord's will. I don't understand why I must continue waiting, but I do so expectantly.

February 17, 1997

I thought I found peace in not pursuing adoption, but lately it is all I think about. Tonight especially. So with the house clean and the dog not begging for his nightly walk, I escape to a candle-lined bathtub. While soft tunes from the

81

radio drown the silence of the house, I am alone to consider my next move.

I'm still foggy about the road that looms ahead of me. The options laid out, I must choose and proceed. This brings me to the possibility of adoption. What does it mean? That I am to love another's child and live in fear that eventually this child will need to find his or her biological mom?

I feel cheated when I think that I'll never look upon a child and say, "She has my nose" or "He has his daddy's smile." I've had hundreds of dreams of what a child of mine might look and act like. I can't give all that up for a baby I would know nothing about. Then I wonder how I would explain his or her behavior. I couldn't say, "She gets that from her daddy"...or could I? Does environment or heredity comprise a child? Suddenly there is something unnatural about adoption, and I sense a hesitation in my soul. Is it God or just plain fear keeping me from going forward?

82

April 29, 1997

It has been a while since I wrote anything because we have faced some dramatic changes. We are changing jobs and moving again, which closes out another chapter of our lives after a very short year. How quickly it escaped our grasp, never to be part of our lives again. I am grateful yet remorseful. Smarter yet sadder. Confused but somehow confident.

This past year consisted of a new job for Regi in a different state and in a new home. New neighbors and friends opened my eyes to a place I never thought twice about. The year saw me through my post-abortion Bible study and handed me the infertility issue. Right when I thought I had it all memorized, the notes changed and I am forced to learn a new song.

I've learned that life and jobs are fleeting and shouldn't be taken so seriously. I thought we could be happy here for a good five years, but now we must start over and move on. Within a year almost to the date, we've pitched a For Sale By Owner sign in the yard and started thumbing through the classified ads. In one whirlwind week we've managed to tidy up various friendships and say good-bye to some we may never see again. The phone rang incessantly the first week, but I expect it to slow down as time passes. This sudden change leaves me a bit angry that my Eiffel Tower of dreams will be reduced to a shambles. My chartered course will now take a new direction.

I had every intention of following through with further surgery this summer. An attempt to open my fallopian tubes seemed the next best thing since I had good insurance and had located a well-known specialist. I planned to volunteer at the crisis pregnancy center and use my newfound

83

freedom and healing to help other women facing unwanted pregnancies. Instead of seeing my dreams through, we are now faced with financial uncertainty, loss of insurance benefits and the task of finding a new place to live. Once again, I will have to make new friends, find another church and plant some more flowers in a flowerbed somewhere.

To the uncertainty, I say that Jesus Christ is the same yesterday, today and forever. Maybe my soul has become like fallow ground and needs a good upheaval. Maybe change is good after all!

I struggle to see how any of this will work out for our good, but I have yet another reason to fully lean on the Lord.

May 12, 1997

Mother's Day is here, and I've had a better day than I imagined. By now I'm used to not receiving one of those hand-painted carnations at church and not standing for a hearty ovation with all the other mothers. No free desserts were offered to me today!

When I woke up, I took a chance to reflect on my past. Part of me wants to celebrate the child I never knew. For a short time I was someone's mother and wish I could proclaim it. I look forward to next Mother's Day when I may possibly be among the honorees. I continue to dream of that first "I love you, Mommy" card and secretly long to pin that dried out carnation to my chest.

May 18, 1997

Mark 11:22-24; Isaiah 40

The answers to my prayers are not always in order, but the strength to overcome every obstacle is always within reach. God's word says I will run yet not grow weary, and walk through valleys filled with death yet not faint. He never said there wouldn't be races or valleys! I long for the day when I will mount up with wings as eagles and find my strength renewed.

I will exercise my right to sing in the night hours, in the moments just before dawn breaks on my lost dreams. I will muster the strength from inside to fly over one more sunset, and find one more joy in the setting sun. His strength is perfect!

June 6, 1997

Life is funny, and if I didn't laugh along with it, it would laugh at me. We feel a release to move to Nashville since an opportunity has opened up there for Regi. Our future is unclear, and I wonder if Regi senses my hesitancy. We are moving out of church ministry into another capacity of ministry, and while part of me is nervous, another part of me is more excited about this than any other opportunity we've ever had. We've always talked about moving to Nashville, and now we are taking that step. I just never knew it would be out of necessity.

I feel like we are starting over in our marriage, working various jobs just to pay the bills. A little hard work never hurt anyone, but it sure is tiring. To make things worse, we just found out we'll be getting new insurance, self-employed, which is pretty expensive. Of course this dashes my hopes for further surgery since I'll be hard pressed to find anyone willing to take on my pre-existing condition. We opted out of maternity benefits since they are quite expensive, so for the first time I'm hoping against pregnancy. Imagine that.

On the way home from the insurance office I cried. It's as though God doesn't want me to ever have children. Am I supposed to give up and give in to my condition? Maybe God isn't the all-powerful person I've been talking about until now. If He were, things would be much different.

My heart grapples with the issue of children. I shudder as I think about the impending answer, afraid of what it will do to me. I've run from it for so long that I'm tired of the race. I am not satisfied with the finality that I will never be a mother; there is no peace for me in those words. I'm exhausted from hurting each time someone else tells me they are pregnant or when another friend tells me she is having a boy. I cannot smile at them anymore or look at one more enlarged belly without going completely mad.

I lay my fleece before the Lord. The question is this, "God, is it Your will for me to ever have a child?" As hard as the words are, I can do nothing else but face the fate and leave it up to God.

July 3, 1997

My prayers have revealed that God does not want to withhold children from me. Praise the Lord! I pray He forgives me for making my anger into an altar. For so long now, my inability to conceive has consumed my life like a storm cloud hovering on the horizon. I forgot how consuming mercy is. Yes, my longing to have children seems to be a hopeless situation, but His mercies are new every morning. This sheds light on my ever-changing situation and gives me the hope I need to persevere.

87

The tears stop for a moment and the pain subsides. I know this won't be the end for I am only human. Then, as if a veil were being yanked from my vision, I catch another glimpse of Jesus. He is not dealing with me according to my sin, nor punishing me for my iniquities. Instead He is allowing me a time of darkness, of reflection, and that is okay. I need it in order to grow in Him. He is preparing me to take flight as a butterfly, beautiful and lovely in His eyes, for a journey only He knows the ending of.

July 5, 1997

I am going to do something for the fist time today—call an adoption agency. I dial the first one I see in the phone book and stumble over every word. Does the woman on the other end already know that I am ignorant on the subject? She leads me through Basic Adoption 101 and tells me what to expect and what not to get my hopes up for. Like the fact that it could take years.

Many babies out there are waiting to be held. Not only do these kids need mommies and daddies, they need love. She continues with options like bi-racial babies, sibling adoptions and adopting an older child. These cases, she says, are the most needy cases.

After only a few minutes, I know I am ready to begin the process. Count me in, sign me up! When she starts talking about money, I say count me out, take my name off the list! It's odd to think I may have to "buy" a baby in order to be a mom. It seems cold and predictable. When I place the receiver back on its cradle, I get tingles all over like some northern wind is steering me away from this path. I pray for peace and direction if we are to pursue this avenue.

July 12, 1997

I began cleaning my new condo today, the deep scouring cleanup of dirt left behind by the former owners. I've arranged most of my stuff the way I like it, the tall vases with the tall, the short with the short, sometimes mingling where necessary. This is my new home, and I intend to make it feel just that—homey.

When I stoop to the level of the dirt and grime, I feel a kinship and am not proud. On days like today, when emotions have risen to a 4.0 on the Richter scale, I am no better than the dirt in front of me. I got into a bad mood today and snapped when Regi said something insignificant. What started out as a tremor became a quake. His touch made me withdraw and sent chills up my spine. The depression is in full swing now, and there is no changing it. Regi takes cover, and the dog follows.

I do my best cleaning when I'm in a foul mood. Probably because the dirt mirrors my soul. So, with abrasives in hand, I tackle the dirt with a vengeance. The cloth immediately turns a dingy yellow with its first swipe. There is more dirt than I imagined, even though it looks clean on first glimpse. I almost give up on the rest of the countertops until I drop the tarnished rag into my clean bucket of water. The water will have to be changed soon.

I am a woman obsessed. I clear the counters, open the window shades, unscrew, unhook—whatever it takes to do a deep-down clean. The windowpane is speckled with yellow dirt from fifteen years' worth of smoking from the past owners. Nicotine has helped itself to my ceiling, walls and floors. I scrape, scrub and pull, determined to allow the natural beauty to shine through.

I am now aggravated. Why did we buy someone else's mess? I didn't ask for it, don't want it and am already sick of it. I work because I have no choice, and it looks like we'll be here a while.

The comparisons grow with each wipe of the rag. Now that I am elbow deep into the process, I can't quit, nor can I escape the grime. My heart is no better than the window lock I've rescued from its dirty place. It is sticky with some brownish substance I don't care to know more about. Even the screws that held it in place have the disease. At first I wouldn't have touched the foreign substance, but now I don't care. In order to clean it, I must be familiar with it. How else will I know when it is gone?

Perhaps the reason I work with such vigor is because I am purging my heart at the same time. I am no better than the countertops that appear clean until I look underneath. To many people I must look clean. On the surface that is. Yet hidden among my manicured nails and perfectly applied make-up the dirt has hardened for years. I know this because I have been forced to live in its decaying ruin.

Bitterness, unforgiveness and lovelessness have given way to the filth in the corners of my soul. Even worry has collected itself over the years to become an ugly stain. I've worried that God doesn't know me, or hear me, or even care. Panic has claimed its spot beneath the yellowed stains of guilt, condemnation and pity. It has built up, multiplying itself until I can stand the dirt no longer.

God's cleaning process stands to be quite different from the one I used on the condo. First of all, He sees everything, no matter how I try to cover it up. The doubt and uncertainty of having a baby, the anger at Him for not healing me, the times I lash out at Regi–not a single stain is hidden from His view. To clean me up He certainly doesn't use a harsh scouring pad, although I could use it. He gently picks me up, forgives my sin and loves me as if I had never sinned.

I am humbled that I serve a God who has every right to be detested with my faithlessness and sin. And while I won't be dirt free until I reach heaven, I pray that in the future I won't be like the dirt I found today, hidden by my grooming skills and allowed to fester. From now on I will not hide behind a windexed Bible, made only to look good around friends and family. Instead, I want to live with God's Word on my heart so that the dirt of the world cannot build up in me any longer.

It is much nicer living in a clean home anyway.

July 14, 1997

The days can be so lonely when Regi travels. I am alone in our condo, without a single friend. I've been here before and I don't like it! I search for the Lord in the quiet of a brand new morning, before the lights have exercised their freedom, before the coffee is pumped into my veins and before my feet feel their strength this new day.

God is on my mind from the first moment I wake up, and He makes me feel warm and cozy inside. Sometimes I slide between the brushed cotton sheets and look up to heaven and dream about what is waiting for me over there. What comfort to know He watches in return, and even takes the time to spend such a sweet moment with me. My eyes lock on His unseen gaze, and I don't have to say anything. He already knows my every thought.

In the stillness, when all I hear is the low whir of the ceiling fan and the hollow ticking of the clock, I feel like a caterpillar deep in its cocoon who waits patiently for the moment it can find his new life. It is not a bad place to be, the quiet of life, waiting on God. Right now I may not be entitled to any answers, and that is all right too. I'm still growing.

Yes, there are doors I wish would open, but maybe I'm not ready to enter that crowded room. I actually enjoy being alone, free to contemplate and dream unhindered. The caterpillar doesn't question. It just settles into its cocoon until its body has developed wings and it is transformed into a colorful new creature.

> *No discipline seems pleasant at the time, but painful. Later on, however, it produces a harvest of righteousness and peace for those who have been trained by it.*
>
> —Hebrews 12:11, NIV

93

> *And my God will meet all your needs according to his glorious riches in Christ Jesus.* —Philippians 4:19, NIV

> *Be my rock of refuge, to which I can always go; give the command to save me, for you are my rock and my fortress.* —Psalm 71:3

September 15, 1997

My pen has been silent for some time now. Neither my passion nor my desire has faded; they've just lost their steam. Much has happened with the move. I can successfully say that I've mastered the art of change! We are praying about Regi branching out into a solo ministry that we've always dreamed of but never thought possible. God has opened a door of opportunity, which will come with great sacrifice. We're both going back to work, which I am not looking forward to. It might, however, fill my loneliness and idle time.

Since I last journaled, a momentous occasion took place: my thirtieth birthday. It came and went without fanfare, but with great attention from Regi. He is good to me.

I placed great anticipation on August 25, 1997. How many times did I say in the past, "I don't want to be thirty years old and just starting a family"? I always earmarked thirty as the age when I would either have it together or still be trying to get it together. Whatever state I found myself in would dictate the rest of my life. Now that I've rounded that corner, I realize I am better equipped to conquer anything that should come my way, as opposed to even five years ago.

I still trust and believe God for my healing. While there are times I fight the urge to shy away from my belief, I root myself in God's Word. I feel abandoned at times, and then I am broken to tears. I shake my fist, turn from God and question what kind of Father would allow me to be infertile. Why does He watch me suffer when He is able to supply? Is He powerless instead of powerful? Unforgiving instead of forgiving? Stingy instead of generous?

It is odd how I entertain such thoughts when I already know the answer. He loves me and has a plan for me that includes powerful blessings, unconditional forgiveness and divine provision.

Because of the many changes we've endured so far, I can't help but admit that God's timing has been perfect. The financial setback we've incurred by moving to Nashville is immense. We struggle to make ends meet, and I can't imagine having a child to provide for right now. I still haven't made any friends and am alone for much of the week while Regi travels. A baby would not fit into the scheme of things at this moment.

95

October 15, 1997

Another new chapter in our saga has officially begun. Regi and I both started back to work this week. I'm working retail. Need I say more?

I am qualified to do something a bit more challenging, but our situation forces us to this outlet. Since we only have one car, we can't work too far from one another and constantly be in contention about who drives and who picks up. Besides, we live ten minutes from the mall and convenience plays a big factor. Every day on the way to work I reassure myself that I'll be able to walk away from my job without any ties.

It is nice to be around other women, and I have made a few friends along the way.

December 27, 1997

The days pass quickly, as evidenced by the encroaching New Year that will soon be upon us. If I ever thought time would wait for me, I was wrong. It waits for no one.

In its passing, I've seen my choices narrowed, decisions forced and futures determined. There are times, single moments frozen in the busyness of the day, when I see God in everything, hear Him in every sound. Other times I can't find Him anywhere. I know He is there; I must search for Him. Some days I don't have the strength, others I don't have the will.

I am terrified of what may never be. I may never be a mother. We may never be a family. The dream is distancing itself from me more every day. A knot settles deep in my stomach, and I remind myself to be strong and take courage. I must remain hopeful.

December 29, 1997

> *"Forget the former things; do not dwell on the past. See, I am doing a new thing!*
>
> *Now it springs up; do you not perceive it? I am making a way in the desert and streams in the wasteland."*
>
> —Isaiah 43:18-19, NIV

January 1, 1998

Happy New Year! Time has passed as quickly as the sand that streams through the proverbial hourglass. Where did the year slip?

1997 saw a great deal of change in our lives. In a way, I am glad it has finally ended, although I don't know how much can change just because the seven has become an eight. For the lack of any other reason, today signifies new beginnings. A new year means new starts and fresh outlooks. Now is the time for me to change my attitude and focus.

When I recap my year, I chuckle. Life has kept me guessing! The year started out the same as usual with the house, job and dog...steady and on course. I enjoyed staying home, helping Regi at church, going to Bible study and singing in the choir. Midway through the year, Regi's sudden job change, the For Sale sign in the front yard, weeks of not knowing who would send the next paycheck. Then the new job, the sold sign and the moving van. We settled, had another job change or two and developed a new routine. Things are much different now as we are both working and trying to get Regi's ministry calendar booked in our extra time.

The infertility still looms over me like a dark cloud that has settled in for a long day's rain. At times I've felt like it was about to burst and shower answers to my questions, while at other times it continues to hover.

I am at peace and determined to view it differently, starting today. First I will pray whether or not this is my season. Maybe I should put away my desires for a while and concentrate on what God has intended for me this upcoming springtime. Walking through the mall yesterday, I began reciting scriptures about healing. Maybe it is time for the victory season–to stop asking and start receiving. To stop crying and start laughing. To stop worrying and start believing.

This upcoming year may not produce utter bliss, but I will get through it with His grace. I look forward to what this season in my life holds and all the seasons to follow. There is much uncharted territory to explore, and I look forward to welcoming a new dawn.

March 4, 1998

Outside the winter has slowly given up its rites to spring. The frost-hardened ground has begun to soften so that yellow daffodils and white lilies can make their glorious ascent. The seasons are changing.

Today I saw Dr. James F. Daniell, M.D., an infertility specialist. It is funny how the scenery changes in these doctors' offices, but the jittery feeling in my stomach remains the same. I waited alone in the examining room and contemplated what this doctor would say to shed any light upon my situation. He is supposed to be one of the best in his field.

Once in his office, the news was optimistic. He told me he is certain he can help and is willing to try to repair/open my fallopian tubes. This is my decision because I want to do everything possible to obtain a natural pregnancy. He won't know the extent of the damage until he looks at my tubes during another laparoscopy. Here we go again! He also asked if I would like to be part of a study to try out a new product that may help promote healing within, thus preventing further adhesion forma-tions. I will get monetary compensation, which will help with the doctor's bill since my insurance will pay only 50 percent of the operation.

99

Many emotions still swirl within me, and it is difficult not to get my hopes up for fear that the operation will be a complete flop. It has been a long ride getting here, yet I'm determined to go the full distance. These past few weeks, I've managed not to let the infertility issue cloud over what else has been happening in our lives. Regi is finally completing his CD project, my sister Monica has moved in with us, and God is providing for our needs. Rest comes easy during this chosen season of my circumstance; I believe that a new season, one of favor, is inviting me into its midst.

March 9, 1998

Today I plan to call Dr. Daniell and schedule the procedure. I am ready to go forward in great anticipation. I pray for the finances to cover the rest of the procedure because it could cost well into the thousands just for our part. I waiver on whether or not to even go through with this since we really don't need the added expense. Then I realize that if God is opening these doors for the surgery to happen, He will come through with the financing. If faith can be selective, mine certainly is! To contradict my thoughts, I read Numbers 11:23 where it asks if the Lord's arm has been shortened. And Numbers 13:30 that says to "go up at once and take possession, for we are able to overcome it." That is the kind of faith I need!

100

March 12, 1998

Tonight I am restless. One thought after another races through my mind, so I start to write. It always helps. There are times when talking to someone just doesn't fulfill the need as writing and praying does.

I can't get the impending operation off my mind tonight. It is way too early to start feeling anxious, but I can't help it. Will the darkness get a bit darker before my dawn creeps in? I do not know. The more I think about this next step of correcting my infertility, the more I question my motives. What am I trying to do? Change the hand I've been dealt? Deter the will of God? Am I supposed to allow His supernatural healing and leave doctors out of this? The questions bounce around my head like jumping beans in full action. On top of everything, in order to be part of the study, I must allow Dr. Daniell to do another laparoscopy eight weeks after this one so he can document the outcome of the product. Just call me a glutton for punishment. The worst possible scenario would be an unsuccessful surgery that leaves me in no better shape than I am now. I view it as having nothing to lose and a baby to gain.

101

I fight tonight's fear that grips me by reading scriptures and praying. God has not given me a spirit of fear! I want to cry out in desperation, but I muzzle my gasps. They will not help. One part of me counts down toward my surgery set for April 29, another wants to erase it from the calendar. Why do I want to put myself through the pain again? Maybe I am experiencing pain so that the joy will be greater one day. Today I mourn, but tomorrow I will dance.

March 16, 1998

Today has been a roller-coaster day. I made the mistake of conducting personal business at work and am sorry I opened that can of worms!

In an attempt to finalize my surgery options, I called the hospital to inquire about the fees I will incur as a result of my operation. The damage? A whopping $3,000 just for the hospital, of which I will be responsible for half. On the day of the operation I must present $500 as a down payment, which won't even include the physician or anesthesiologist's fee. When I heard those words, I could hardly find enough air in my lungs to launch another breath. We simply are not able to incur yet another bill.

On that note, I left to go home for lunch and broke out into tears even before I unlocked the car door. I can't make sense of how I am feeling, except that I should probably cancel the surgery and be happy with my lot in life. Why do I insist on putting myself through yet another feeble attempt at the unknown? I crumble inside from anger of all I've ever done to wind up in this mess. I curse my stupidity, my financial uncertainty, my body for not working right, God, everything. Then I curse myself for blaming God and start the vicious cycle all over again. I can't stand this state I am in!

I wonder if I should just give in to the infertility and start grieving for the children I will never have.

Later, when Regi called to check in on me, I fought to hide my panic. I told him the discouraging news about the cost of the operation, to which he responded, "Kim, where's your faith in what God can do from now until then? A whole month is but a second to God, and He doesn't need that long to work it all out."

I blew it again by stepping in and taking the reins out of the Lord's hands in order to do my own steering. And to think it would take my husband, who probably doesn't even want me to have this operation, to turn my thinking around. Sure, he knows how badly I want to go through with the surgery, but he could agree with me and cancel the whole thing.

March 19, 1998

103

Three days since my "lapse into oblivion." I have put off writing in my journal only because I need to retract my whole last entry. Who was that "doubting Thomasina?"

It is times like these that I wonder if I have to start all over again in my cycle of faith. I look forward to my surgery on April 29 because somehow, someway, God is going to perform a miracle.

We sang a song called "Enemy's Camp" at church on Sunday. What timing. I've had enough of Satan mulling over my situation, holding me hostage and roasting me over a blazing fire. I stormed his camp and took back everything he took from me, once and for all!

Adoption

April 9, 1998

Just when I thought I had everything figured out, something else has come along to throw me into a tailspin. Regi called this morning from out of town where he is part of a four-day revival. He began by telling me how everything went in the services the night before and how he had been having such a wonderful time with Pastor Joe Wright, a newfound friend. Then he told a story that has left my mind reeling and my heart thumping so loudly I can't concentrate on anything else around me.

It actually started when Regi and Pastor Joe met almost a year ago, after we first moved to Nashville. He and Pastor Joe struck up a conversation at a concert when he was traveling as the accompanist to a Christian recording artist. Their conversation turned to marriage, kids and future dreams. I don't know why it came about, but Regi told him of my upcoming laparoscopy and our bout with infertility. It turns out that Pastor Joe and his wife experienced a similar problem twenty-five years ago and ended up adopting a baby girl. After their lengthy discussion, Pastor Joe invited Regi as a mucis guest at his church. At the time Regi didn't think this pastor was serious because not only were they complete strangers, but Pastor Joe had never heard Regi sing or play.

Regi left this past Saturday to be in their services and is having a wonderful time. He even met up with some friends we knew from New York who now live in the city he is visiting. They came to the service on Sunday night to see Regi and also brought some friends who recently adopted a baby.

The next evening after his concert, while Regi was signing CDs at the product table, a man asked him to sign the CD to his children. Actually, he said, it was for his son and daughter who happened to be adopted.

105

On Tuesday, Regi met up with our friends from New York again and drove over to meet their minister of music before enjoying lunch together. Once again, the conversation went on to discuss each other's wives, children and everything in between. This man and wife were in a similar infertility situation as ours but were due to adopt a baby in another month.

I tuned in and out as Regi spoke since I was trying to get dressed for work. I stopped applying mascara the second he told me how this whole story involved us. Wednesday at lunch, Pastor Joe approached Regi with a serious question. He said he didn't know where we stood with our infertility but that God had placed us in his mind when a member of the church approached him the night before. Her name is JoAnn Peckham, and she and her husband handle private adoptions. She asked him if he knew anyone who wanted to adopt a baby boy because she was looking for a Christian family to be considered. Pastor Joe said we came to his mind first and suggested Regi call JoAnn before returning home.

The next day, Regi called JoAnn. She told him about a baby she was trying to place who was due to be born on May 8. Regi said there was no way that could be a possibility for us. He figured their conversation was over. "Hold on," she said, "I'm also trying to place another baby who isn't going to be born until July. Would you like me to try and arrange a meeting with the birth parents before you leave?" His response stunned me. He told JoAnn yes!

Little did I know that while I lay in bed on Wednesday evening, he was sharing a soda with two seventeen-year-olds who were searching for parents to adopt their baby. They loved the baby she was carrying but clearly weren't ready for the responsibility of raising a child. They asked Regi every question imaginable, and he answered them the best he could. They shared their hearts and took notes. They would gladly consider us to be the parents of this baby.

As Regi relayed the story to me, I sobbed. I don't know if he sensed the tears streaming down my face or heard the change in my voice, but I didn't want him to know my excitement until I knew where this was headed. I simply could not believe what I was hearing. The man on the other end of the phone sounded like my husband, but something was different. He didn't do this for me; he did it for himself.

After their meeting, Regi returned to his hotel to contemplate what had just occurred. He didn't call me because it was so late and he knew I had to wake up early for work. When he called me this morning, he had already spoken with JoAnn, who said the birth parents were extremely interested in us. They simply wanted more information on me. She told him not to pursue this avenue if we weren't definitely interested, because things looked good so far. She said the birth father responded to Regi better than he had to anyone else.

107

He then told me to think about whether or not I wanted to pursue this avenue. Think? There was no thinking needed. As if God were whispering in my ear, I suddenly knew this baby girl would be mine.

April 12, 1998

Ever since Regi arrived home, I've bombarded

him with questions. What did they look like? Are they sure about what they're doing? Tell me their exact words!

I couldn't stay focused at work, nor could I tell anyone what was on my mind. Too often have I told people about some impending good news only to go back and explain why it didn't happen. Of course my sister Monica knows, and we have agreed to pray and wait on the Lord.

This could very well be the day we hear back from Scott and Rebecca. Two days ago we overnighted photographs of our families and us. I wrote a letter to Rebecca telling her in my own words how much this all means to me. I know they won't make a decision in a day, but I wish I knew how they felt.

Here's what I wrote to her:

Dear Rebecca,

I wanted to enclose a special note just from me to you. I can't imagine what you are feeling as you are preparing to make one of the greatest decisions of your life. You are showing the kind of strength I long for, and selflessness that deserves to be applauded. The love you have for your baby shows in that you are doing everything possible to find the most perfect family for her to be part of.

When I found out about my infertility, I thought my world had ended. I felt like I was cheating my husband out of one of the greatest joys that life could afford us as a couple. I thought I was worth nothing. When I was alone, I cried because I thought no one knew how I felt. One of my greatest dreams had been crushed and I didn't know where I would get the strength to go on. But God has been faithful and made me even stronger through this situation. I now live with the confidence that God is going to bless us with many children, in His timing, and with the exact children He has planned for us.

While struggling with infertility has made me quite emotional, I really thought I had cried every available tear in my body. However, when Regi told me that we were going to be among those considered to be your little girl's parents, I cried and cried and cried! I've prayed for so long that Regi and I would be blessed with a baby, but I never dreamed it could happen. For the first time in a while, I see how possible it is that we will be someone's Mommy and Daddy one day, even if it isn't to your baby. I've always felt like my infertility was the consequence for everything wrong I ever did, but for the first time I realize how hopeful our future is and how God can work miracles in very mysterious ways!

Please know above all that whether or not you choose Regi and I, it is my hope that you do not only what is best for your little girl, but for you and Scott also. I pray that you will find peace in your choice of parents,

and that you gain the wisdom you need to make this decision. You can rest assured every night before you go to sleep that if we are your choice, your baby will be loved unconditionally. And not only by us but also by wonderful great-grandparents, grand-parents, aunts, uncles and cousins who are just waiting to love a new baby. My arms have longed to be filled with a baby for so long that I just don't know if I would ever let go of her!

If you have any other questions or concerns, you may call us at any time. We are truly honored that you've even decided to consider us. You have given me yet another moment's strength and another day's hope. I promise to pray for you in the months to come and in the lifetime that is ahead of you. May your years be filled with peace, love and happiness.

With love and prayers.

To say I'm a little overwhelmed would be an understatement. As soon as the package went into the mail chute, a feeling of "What am I doing?" flooded over me. It's hard to imagine that this may actually come through. The more I allow myself to ponder all the repercussions, the more I convince myself that I don't deserve this good fortune and will never pull this one off.

I know, however, that God is watching over this

whole situation and it never would have come to pass had He not intended it. His grace will allow me to get through these next few days of sheer nervousness as I wait to hear from the birth parents. He also will strengthen me if it all ends in disappointment. I pray that if this is not the Lord's will He deter us quickly, change our minds or put an obstacle in the way. I would rather know before we get too emotionally involved.

It is impossible not to get excited in this situation. I wasn't going to tell my family, but I broke down and called them all with the possibility. We cried and laughed together, and they are now as anxious as we are. To top it off, Regi asked what I would name the baby! I can't believe this is the man I've been married to for the last eight years. He is actually excited about adopting this baby girl. I am encouraged by his feelings, and it gives me hope, even if this doesn't come through. For the first time ever, I feel his sincere desire to become a father. I don't know his reasoning for wanting to adopt so badly, but he is adamant. It heals my heart to see this part of him. Now I know that anything is possible with God!

111

For now, I will go to work and check my messages every five minutes to see if JoAnn has called. This process has given me a new outlook on my infertility: there is hope. I trust God for whatever He is preparing for us.

April 13, 1998

The waiting is the hardest part. Subconsciously I've put my life on hold, and I am looking at everything differently. It is as though my whole life is before me, but I can't take part in it because it could possibly change.

Regi and I have spoken with JoAnn numerous times, and she is clearly optimistic about the outcome. While my faith does not rest in her, I have this overwhelming respect for her. Just this morning when I called her, she was so encouraging with her words and her gentle spirit. What an awesome job God has placed before her. I am thankful He placed her in our path.

JoAnn did say that in addition to more than twenty couples being considered, one more couple has entered the scene. They are friends of Rebecca's guidance counselor at school whom she promised to consider before making any final decision. My mind drifts in curiosity as to who they are, what they do and whether or not they are "better" than us. Sad to admit but true. This becomes a competition, and a baby is the prize. Now the answer we thought we could have by Saturday may be prolonged until Wednesday. As my sister put it last night, it's like being in the Miss America Pageant and waiting to see who gets the crown.

The unfortunate part in this whole debate is

that many people, possibly myself and Regi, will be turned away and left to wonder what more they could have said, what else they could have done. It is impossible not to take the rejection personally, but I will if we are turned down. I know my appearance, financial status, the way I talk—everything—is under a microscope. Maybe it's a good thing that everything came together in such a hurry so I didn't have too much time to think about what to wear, what to say and how to act.

Now I wonder if I jumped the gun in telling my family and a few friends about the possible adoption. They continue to call to see if we have found anything out, which makes matters worse. But they are my family and will share our joy or help us get through the disappointment. They have waited so long for a baby!

113

April 14, 1998

Tuesday morning. The wait continues. I am about to leave for work soon, which is good since my mind is preoccupied with the impending ringing of the telephone. I can't stand it!

My devotion time this morning included the passage from Luke 17:6: "If you have faith as small as a mustard seed, you can say to this mulberry tree, 'Be uprooted and planted in the sea,' and it will obey you." I, like the apostles in verse 5, say, "Increase my faith!"

I feel good today and rest in the revelation that I am in the Lord's hand. No matter the outcome. Wasn't it me who said that God wouldn't give me something I couldn't handle? Oh yeah!

What I do know is that I need increasing faith as the days go by. Mom said last night in one of her pep talks that I should revisit my childhood and have the faith of my youth. That is, faith that doesn't worry about where my next meal will come from, or whether or not I'll have somewhere to lay my head. My table was always full and the bed was always warm.

If I don't leave it in God's hands, I'll go crazy. Only faith keeps me pressing in to the Lord, and only He will get me through the days ahead.

April 15, 1998

It is 7:30 a.m. and I am up alone. I wonder if the answer will find us today or if we will be forced to stay in limbo a while longer. What are they doing on the other end? I assure myself that decisions like this warrant time and great consideration. I do want the birth parents to be absolutely sure rather than change their minds after selecting their baby's parents. As with any adoption, there is the risk of something happening right down to the second a baby is born.

On a realistic scale, I can't imagine being chosen—I've never even won a raffle! Other couples like us are waiting, going through the same emotions we are. If only there were more babies to go around.

My mom called me at work yesterday and asked if I had heard anything. I couldn't believe she would think I'd put off calling her if I had. She and the rest of the family are so excited they can hardly think of anything else. I considered calling JoAnn again yesterday but rationalized that she would call as soon as she knew something.

Today I will act like normal and think peaceful thoughts. I must get through the day with whatever strength I can muster. May God's will be done.

April 16, 1998

The news came at 11 o'clock last night, just as we crawled into bed. I had resigned my heart to not being chosen so it wouldn't hurt so badly if the news didn't turn out in our favor. Protection, I guess. When the phone rang, I knew it had to be JoAnn since no one else ever calls so late at night. Regi answered and kept pretty calm so I wouldn't suspect it was her. I lay there frozen, afraid to breathe, until I knew the outcome. Regi wasn't screaming, so I didn't know what to think. At first his voice made it sound good, then it sounded not so good. My heart raced as he handed the phone to me. I heard the sweetest words I've ever imagined.

"Congratulations. You are going to be the mommy of this sweet little girl." And the tears started. I kicked and screamed into the phone, an outburst of sheer joy.

Rebecca told JoAnn to tell me not to cry, but that was all I could do. Before I even drifted off to sleep, my dream came true. It was really happening!

Once we hung up the phone, we didn't know what to say. I wanted to jump and scream out all at once. The only thing left to do was call everyone—no matter what time it was. Monica joined our late-night celebration and kept repeating, "I can't believe it." I called everyone in my family and shared my joy. They were elated and speechless. My grandfather and I have had a standing agreement that whenever I found out I was going to have a baby, I was to call him immediately. No matter the time. Imagine his surprise when I took him at his word! After Regi called his family, we savored the joy and thanked God for our miracle.

As I lay in bed unable to sleep, it suddenly occurred to me that if I thought this past week had been excruciating, how in the world was I going to get through the next two and a half months? "Our" baby girl is due on July 3, so time is short. Ten weeks to develop patience. I've already dreamed of what she will look like and what it will feel like to hold her tiny fingers in mine—even what her cry will sound like. Her eye color, her hair color—it all enthralls me, and I just want to hold this blessing close. I can hardly wait to bathe her, wrap her in one of the pink blankets my mom made for her or see my father hold his first grandchild. I wonder what Regi will do when he sees her, or how he will respond to her first cry.

How will I bond with this little girl I've yet to meet? I've often heard that babies respond immediately to their mother's voice as soon as they are born, which makes me wonder how she will react to mine. Will she be confused, or is it possible she will adjust to me as her new mommy without any problem? I've even heard that it is possible to breastfeed an adopted baby, and I am going to look into it immediately. Wouldn't that complete the picture!

My mind drifts to so many different tangents that it is impossible to follow them all. I hope I will be a good parent and adequately provide for her needs. Will I know how to discipline? What kind of a role model will I be? Will the mothering instinct come naturally?

April 17, 1998

It is safe to say I've told everyone about the baby—whether they wanted to hear it or not!

People look at me blankly, utterly shocked, when I tell them since this is a complete surprise for everyone. It would be one thing to say I was pregnant and had nine months to go, but when I tell them two and a half months they can't believe it. It is difficult not to chatter incessantly about all the preparations, but not everyone wants to hear details of what theme the nursery will be or my plans to buy a car seat. I'm grateful for my co-workers, who have taken such an interest and ask me questions throughout the day.

Three people at work have told me their stories of being adopted. There is this common bond invisibly knit between people adopting and those adopted. They have a little more joy, admiration and respect for what we are doing. It isn't something I can put my finger on, but I feel honored to be among their ranks.

April 18, 1998

Instead of referring to the baby as "she" all the time, it dawned on me that we ought to go ahead and name her. What an important and permanent decision! She will be called by this name the rest of her life, and I will speak the word no less than a million times in my lifetime. Where do we begin?

I've turned the task over to the people around me. The girls at work bombard me daily with their newest ideas. I asked Monica and my other sister,

Annalisa, Regi, my parents, everyone to come up with their favorite name. Now I find myself going around all day reciting names to myself to see what fits. I know when I hear it, it will click.

April 20, 1998

It took only two short days to come up with the name. Monica chose her favorite—Taylor. Regi likes Madison. I want Sophia.

Then Annalisa called today and left a message on my answering machine saying she had come up with the perfect name for the baby and to call her immediately. I could hardly stand it so I called her as soon as I got home. With bated breath I waited to hear her idea—Sophia.

119

I couldn't believe it! I knew there was something to this "coincidence" and felt that same sense of knowing as before that our baby would be known as Sophia Renee.

April 21, 1998

We set up a phone meeting between myself, Regi, Rebecca and Scott. It is for the benefit of Rebecca and me since we want to meet so badly. I am nervous beyond explanation and have no idea what I'll say.

My heart thumped as Regi dialed the number. Although I knew they were on the other end, I thought that perhaps they were out or had changed their minds about talking. Once Scott answered, he and Regi made small talk. When Regi handed me the phone I heard Rebecca's voice, as timid as mine, on the other end. We also made small talk at first, and then found ourselves laughing and sharing about Sophia. She loves the name, by the way, and seems very much at ease about us adopting her baby. I didn't know how she would respond, but I think she likes me! I pray she feels peace about us because I want her to rest soundly every night of her life in the knowledge that we are taking wonderful care of this special part of her.

120

Rebecca is going to send the sonogram of Sophia that she just had taken, maybe even the one of her sucking her thumb. I can hardly wait to catch a glimpse of our baby!

What a blessing to be on the receiving end of this whole process. I know it is all going to end well and that Sophia will be with us soon. What a fortunate baby to have two mothers who love her so much. I am grateful to Rebecca for keeping her safe and warm until the day she is placed into our arms. I am also thankful that Rebecca is committed to taking care of herself through prenatal visits to her doctor and by doing all the other precautionary stuff pregnant women do. I cannot imagine how hard it is for her to carry a baby for nine months only to give her to someone else. It is bravery that I, sad to say, never had. It is not that she doesn't love this baby; it is that she loves this baby so much. Once again, I give thanks to the Lord for showing favor on us.

April 26, 1998

Sophia, I said a prayer for you, my little one. I will not allow a day to go by that I don't ask Jesus to be where you are, growing you into the perfect child He created you to be. I pray that even today the lullaby of angels would take you off to sleep and that whispers from the heavenlies would gently cradle you until I am able to. I yearn for the moment when our eyes will meet, making us mother and daughter. I wish you were here now!

Today is yet another day that I marvel in the workings of the Lord to get Sophia here. I give in to fear now and again, as to where all the finances will come from for the adoption, and I contemplate my upcoming surgery in a different light now. Do I still want to go through with it, or is this my sign to let it rest? The cost of the surgery plus the cost of the adoption will be more than our budget can sustain, so I pray for some definitive answers.

If I cancel my surgery altogether, I will never be able to rest knowing I haven't done everything to correct my infertility. I view the fact that the insurance will cover 50 percent of the surgery as my sign that I should continue as planned. If I wait even a year, I'll have not only myself and Regi to look after, but also a baby to think about. The questions soak my mind and I need divine confirmation one way or the other. I am so confused!

"Faith is the substance of things hoped for, the evidence of things unseen" (Heb. 11:1). Say no more! It is not for me to fear, for the Lord will bring me through.

April 27, 1998

This morning at work I slipped into panic mode when I picked up my thought process from last night. The only thing I could figure to do was call Dr. Daniell and ask his opinion of what I should do in light of our impending adoption. When I did, he confirmed that the whole procedure could cost up to $5,000, with $2,500 being our part. He graciously said he would forego whatever the insurance wouldn't cover on his part and understood my hesitancy. There would be no pressure from him if I changed my mind.

I even asked a couple of girls at work to pray that God would give me wisdom to make the right decision—to operate or not to operate. Their response was to put it in the Lord's hands and then walk away. Let God be God! How easy to say, but hard to do. I keep feeling that God has brought me to this place and know He won't abandon me now. Once again I wonder if God is just going to open up heaven and send the money down.

Then I decided to call the insurance company to get answers on exactly how much everything would cost. By this time, I knew I would be approved and ready to go, so they would have any information needed to process my request. Baptist Hospital had already told me I would be responsible for $500 up front and then billed for the rest later. It was up to the insurance company on how much I would be billed.

The adjuster pulled up my paperwork, and I gritted my teeth as she read off my information. She had it all in front of her: date of the operation, procedure, everything. Even down to how much coverage I had been approved for. She was about to say the words that would make or break my date with the operating room.

I thought she had pulled up the wrong account, because when she said I was pre-approved for 100 percent coverage of the operation, my heart stopped for a second and the blood drained from my face. It couldn't be. Not wanting to raise her concern from my shock, I casually placed the phone back on the receiver and then called Dr. Daniell's office. The nurse confirmed the same thing—the insurance company had agreed to cover the entire cost of my laparoscopy, not 50 percent like they originally told me.

I wanted to run up the aisles and shout for joy, sing at the top of my lungs, dance with anyone who came my way. I immediately called Regi and told him what I had just found out. He could hardly believe it and reassured me that God was in control of everything. When would I ever catch on that God is in control of all things and works everything out in His perfect timing!

April 28, 1998

Everything is set for my operation, and once again my mom is coming to be with me. Since my last surgery was so trying, Regi pleaded with her to return to my bedside. This would give us the opportunity to work on getting some things together for Sophia at the same time. Everything is working out for good.

April 29, 1998

Mom and Regi escorted me to the hospital for my outpatient surgery in the same way we did last time. I know what to expect this time and am excited about having my fallopian tubes corrected. I can finally rest in the knowledge that I've done everything to correct my infertility. The rest will be up to God.

While we were sitting in the pre-op room, I told Regi and Mom that I had an odd fear of dying from this procedure. Not the type of fear that comes from not trusting God, but the anxious fear that doesn't want to do anything to jeopardize meeting my daughter in another two months. She has quickly changed my perspective on life. Deep down I know that God has great things in store for us as a family and that He won't take it from us now.

Lying on the operating table felt similar to the last time I had a laparoscopy. The prep work, waiting, doctors, nurses and needles were all the same. What a somber time as I floated into my drug-induced sleep and relied on the doctor to correct my infertility and perhaps up the ante on my getting pregnant someday. I fell asleep before I counted to three.

125

When I woke up, I heard the faint voice of a nurse trying to rouse me. I wanted to tell everyone to be quiet and let me sleep, but I could barely utter a sound. The procedure was over, and because of my promise of Sophia, I did not dread waking up. All I heard was some nurse saying she needed to track down Regi and my mom.

Dr. Daniell successfully opened both fallopian tubes, although he was not very pleased with the left side. In eight more weeks when he goes back in for a second look he will most likely fuse that one together so it doesn't pose a threat to any future pregnancies. The right tube is "healthy and pink," as he put it, and ready for action. He gives me a 30 percent chance of a natural pregnancy, better than no chance, and I am encouraged and confident with what I have to work with now. A calm comes in knowing the truth.

April 30, 1998

Today is the day after my surgery and I feel great. Mom and Regi are staying close by to catch me if I pass out or get sick. I've told them I don't have time to be sick and that only one thing is on my mind. They can't believe I am doing so well.

126

The focus has turned to Sophia's arrival, and today we are going to register at the baby store. Nothing could possibly hold me back from picking out diapers, bibs, sheets, pacifiers and anything I will need. I am determined to be ready in case Sophia decides to come early.

This week I met with a lactation consultant at the hospital who is studying the effects of medication, natural herbs and breast pumping to help women nurse adopted babies. The regimen is quite intense and will demand great effort and time on my part. There is no guarantee that I will produce milk, but many women have been successful. Since I spoke with her, I have not come up with one reason why I wouldn't want to go through with this therapy and have already gotten a prescription for the pills I will be taking. Everything is falling into place, and soon I will be a mother. I can hardly stand the wait.

May 1, 1998

One of Regi's concerts got cancelled at the last minute, much to his surprise. We felt this was an opportunity God had put into our path to help with the adoption finances. But due to uncontrollable circumstances, it has been postponed and we are forced to keep believing for a miracle.

After finding out, Regi asked how we would make up for the loss. My answer? Get on the phone and keep calling churches. I feel a confidence that God is going to supply all our needs and we don't need to fear. I think I have finally learned to trust the Lord. I simply refuse to balk at little things like finances when God has done so much (who is this talking?). He will continue to make a way.

127

May 10, 1998

Mother's Day. A day I used to dread. I should be celebrating as a mother-to-be or something! Actually, I have celebrated because Annalisa sent me a basket of baby items that really caught me off guard and made me quite emotional. Then Regi bought me a beautiful robe with matching silk pajamas to stay in the spirit of things. Who ever thought Mother's Day could be so sweet?

Church was wonderful, and I was more emotional than ever. I am quick to blame my raging hormones for my mood swings, but these tears were out of pure gratitude for what is to come. The children's choir sang, and I couldn't contain myself. I was enamored by the innocence of a child, waving from the platform and trying to stand out front so her white patent leathers would be seen. Small eyes scanned the crowd to make sure Mom and Dad were pleased. I can't wait to see Sophia up there one of these days!

The clincher this Mother's Day was when I received a package from Scott and Rebecca. I could hardly catch my breath when I took out the Precious Moments figurine of a mother rocking a baby. I cried, of course, and marveled at the strength these kids have found. This is one gift I will treasure forever.

May 11, 1998

Today I saw the first picture of Sophia inside her birth mother's womb. No words exist to describe what came over me. To see her curled up in that tiny cocoon, resting peacefully, unaware of everyone peering into her hiding place. I already think she is beautiful and looks a little like—well, it is too soon to know that!

May 19, 1998

I spoke with Rebecca last night and it felt like I was talking to one of my sisters. The Lord has blessed our talks together, and I remain grateful that He continues to draw us together. He is so good.

The countdown is somewhere around seven weeks now. My thoughts focus on whether or not Sophia will have a head full of black hair like Rebecca or Scott's naturally curly hair. Who knows, maybe Sophia and I will have matching curls. Her eyes will be brown, green or a cross between. I'm holding out for green.

The breastfeeding process is coming along smoothly. I get very tired throughout the day, a side effect of the medication. I don't mind suffering because the end result will be to nurse Sophia. The hormones I am on are pretty powerful, and I know Regi will be grateful for the day I go off them.

129

Some friends from Memphis gave me a "pseudo-shower" this past weekend. Instead of gifts, however, they blessed us with cash. I never imagined they would even go that far. I am grateful that God sends us friends in our time of need. The truth is, I've always dreamed of a baby shower just for me with decorations, hats, balloons, friends all around. We're so new to Nashville that I figured we would celebrate quietly without any friends.

Yet once again everything has fallen into place perfectly. Friends have doubly blessed us across the many states we've called home along the years. I've had one shower so far, with four more on the way. Besides, my mom, dad, sisters, grand-parents and other family members have bought enough clothes to outfit Sophia's first whole year! Even the girls at work, the place I cursed not so long ago, are taking part. Now I know one of the reasons God put me there.

I trust Him for a healthy, beautiful, gentle-natured baby who is full of Jesus! I have confidence that all is going to go well because He orchestrates everything, not us. He didn't bring us this far to leave us, and He will complete the work He started.

May 25, 1998

Today I am at peace. There is actually peace in waiting. Imagine that! Today is Grandma Crisafulli's birthday, and I hope she celebrates with a bit more joy the way a first time great-grandmother should. I can hardly wait to place Sophia into her arms.

I read from John 14:27, "My peace I give to you; not as the world gives do I give to you. Let not your heart be troubled neither let it be afraid." And John 15:11, "This I have spoken to you, that my joy may remain in you, and that your joy may be full."

The idea that Rebecca or Scott might change their minds about going through with the adoption pops into my mind every now and then, but it's a fleeting thought because of the confidence God has given me. From all the talks we've had, I know Scott and Rebecca are sure about this decision. I'm open and honest each time I speak with Rebecca, and I always ask whether she is having second thoughts. She remains firm in her decision and actually seems excited for us. The relationship we've started is one I will never be able to replace because of the bond we share as mothers. I wish I had her strength.

June 8, 1998

I am up early today, awakened by the soft chirping of birds outside my window. How wonderful to hear life all around. I am comforted by the knowledge that soon I will have yet another person to share these tender morning hours with. I am amazed at how God works, as if He is preparing my body for the early feedings and diaper changes. I am rested and ready to face the challenges and joys that lie ahead.

131

Sophia's due date is just three short weeks away. In another week, Rebecca will find out whether or not she can be induced. She is hoping for this because she wants Regi and I to be there for the birth. She sounds stronger each time I talk with her, and I am strengthened that she still wants to move forward. I lie awake at night and wonder how she is doing physically and emotionally. I don't mean surface feelings, but deep inside her heart. To me, this adoption is the most precious form of life, although I am on the receiving end. I get to go home with the prize. I wonder if she has contemplated what leaving the hospital without Sophia will be like. I pray God gives the strength she needs when she needs it most.

I can't fathom the extent of her decision. She doesn't have to place this baby for adoption, but she is going to do so willingly. What a parallel between this and when God gave up His only Son, Jesus Christ, for me. Willingly, not begrudgingly. Selflessly, not selfishly. That was the ultimate sacrifice. And even though I've yet to cradle Sophia in my arms, I have done so in my mind a hundred times. As far as I'm concerned, she is already mine.

I stay busy counting the days. The baby's room is almost complete, and my baby shower from the girls at work is drawing near. The days pass quickly and I feverishly plan things like maternity leave (I'm praying I don't have to return), what Sophia will wear home from the hospital and how many diapers I should have on hand.

God is blessing Regi by providing a lot of bookings. He is still so new to being on the road, yet God is providing. We pray that he can quit his retail job before long and just travel. I still don't know where the rest of the money for the adoption fees will come from, but I continue to trust the Lord. He knows!

When the Lord brought back the captives to Zion, we were like men who dreamed. Our mouths were filled with laughter, our tongues with songs of joy. Then it was said among the nations, "The Lord has done great things for them." The Lord has done great things for us, and we are filled with joy. Restore our fortunes, O Lord, like streams in the Negev. Those who sow in tears will reap with songs of joy. He who goes out weeping, carrying seed to sow, will return with songs of joy, carrying sheaves with him.

—**Psalm 126:1-6, NIV**

June 9, 1998

Rebecca called today and said she had "near labor" last night. She thought her water broke at about 11:30 p.m. so she went to the hospital. Turns out she had bladder spurts because of the baby sitting directly on her bladder. By 3:30 a.m. she was back home and relieved. It goes to show how quickly this whole delivery process could be! With that in mind, I silently hope the labor and delivery are stalled, just so I can make sure everything is in place. The crib is set up, the walls are painted and lacy, pink baby outfits hang in the closet. Physically I am ready, but emotionally—will I ever be?

June 19, 1998

This morning I am restless again. The wait is overwhelming. I spoke with Rebecca yesterday; her doctor pushed the date back a few days to July 7. I did not want to hear that, although there is nothing I can do except wait. Since I've been doing that for two months now, you'd think I would have developed patience by now. How do women who go through the nine months of pregnancy ever make it that long? They must feel the same way I do—full, ready and anxious.

June 25, 1998

Rebecca is officially dilated to one and 50 percent effaced. Her doctor feels she could go anytime this week. This week! I am still anxious, a little nervous, but mostly excited. I am going to be a mommy soon. I dream daily about the moment our eyes meet, when I feed her and nuzzle her face against mine.

June 27, 1998

Still no baby. I dream of her every night though, and that somehow makes me feel she is already here. Her birth consumes my every thought, which makes it difficult to focus on anything else. Work is simply a means to an end at this point, and I cannot concentrate on my obligations when I am there. I jump when the phone rings, expecting to hear, "It's time!" My camera is loaded and ready, my bags are almost packed. I tell myself I'll finish tonight just to be sure.

Annalisa is going to meet up with us, which I am very excited about. Regi and I both want someone there to share the moment with us (and take pictures).

I savor my moments alone, knowing all too well that the quiet times will be limited from here on out. Instead I will spend my time singing, rocking and reading to Sophia. The waiting makes that moment all the more worthwhile.

By the way, God provided all the finances we needed to cover the adoption. I knew He would, I just didn't know how or when. When we least expect it, He smiles on us in the sweetest ways.

July 1, 1998

Still waiting. No baby, but we are closer than ever. Rebecca had a doctor's appointment today and took a fetal stress test. It looks as though she will be induced on Monday, if she doesn't go on her own before then. We've decided to fly out on Saturday, July 4, which gives us a day to visit with Rebecca and Scott before she goes into the hospital on Sunday. I can't wait to meet her face to face, since I know her so well already. We are going to have lunch together on Sunday then go to the hospital together. From there we'll have to wait until Sophia Renee decides to make her debut into this world and our lives.

July 4, 1998

The jet engine gently hums below me. I've been here before. I feel a slight panic overtake me as the plane revs its machinery in preparation for our journey. I dislike flying, but today I feel more peaceful than ever because I know God's plan is unfolding before us. After months of waiting, the time has finally come to go get our baby! Our baby! The thought brings tears to my eyes every time it comes to mind. This will be one Fourth of July I will never forget.

To say I am nervous about meeting Scott and Rebecca is an understatement. Part of me wonders if they will reject us at this late date because of how I really look (pictures are deceiving) or how I am dressed. I picked my clothes carefully, making sure everything was ironed perfectly. I know they won't be looking at the outside, but my nerves have taken over! I fight the urge to make a perfect first impression, because nothing is ever perfect. I hope she goes into labor as soon as we get there so we won't have to wait any longer than planned. As long as Annalisa makes it in time, we'll be fine.

For now, I am going to recline in my seat and rest for a while. I can't wait to meet JoAnn, our angel from the Lord. What relationships have been birthed during this special time!

When the plane touched down, I felt a sense of anticipation sweep over me that could hardly be contained. I wanted to tell everyone I passed what I was doing in their great city so they could join in our celebration.

Once we dropped our stuff off at the place we would be staying for the week, we made arrangements to meet Scott and Rebecca at the restaurant where he worked. The whole way over to the restaurant, my stomach was in knots. I tried to figure out exactly what I would say. Everything I thought of sounded stupid or fake. Was I supposed to hug her or shake her hand? Did I comment on her belly or not mention the baby just yet?

When I first caught sight of Rebecca, she was even cuter in person than she was in her pictures. As usual, she had a wide smile for all, which calmed my nerves immediately. She looked great and was only a little nervous. I couldn't help but eye her protruding belly and think of my precious Sophia tucked away inside.

Scott didn't say much. I wonder how much of that was nerves? Since Regi had met both of them already, it wasn't too difficult making conversation. We all talked and made plans to meet for lunch tomorrow and then go on to the hospital.

Later in the evening we went to a park with JoAnn and her family to see the fireworks display. How awesome to think that what was going on in my mind was being played out for a whole crowd of people. Once we made it to bed, sleep came easily. Annalisa is due to arrive tomorrow, and Sophia will make her stunning entrance on Monday.

July 5, 1998

We awoke to exciting news. Rebecca's water broke during the night, and she is already at the hospital. I barely got through my cup of coffee when it hit me. My knees felt weak and my heart started to flutter. This was the moment I had been waiting years for!

138

I wanted to go to the hospital immediately, but JoAnn told us it would be a while until Rebecca actually delivered. Instead we prepared for the day ahead, kept the phone lines open and prayed for an easy delivery.

By 2 p.m. we were at the airport to pick Annalisa up. Imagine her surprise when we said we only had time to drop her suitcases off before heading to the hospital. Thank you, Lord, for perfect timing! As soon as she got into the car, she began emptying a suitcase full of gifts for Sophia. She is an excited Auntie.

When we pulled up to the hospital, its many

windows loomed over our heads. Somewhere in one of those rooms Rebecca was lying in a bed about to give birth. I could hardly imagine what was going through her mind. Bittersweet joy, I supposed.

JoAnn, Regi, Annalisa and I all approached the automatic doors, armed and ready with camcorders and cameras. We had a bouquet of roses for Rebecca and a box of Kleenex for ourselves. Who knew what the day had in store.

Then came the most awkward time we had faced yet. As we walked through the doors into labor and delivery, we stumbled upon the waiting room—and were faced with about twenty-five of Scott and Rebecca's family and friends. Mothers, fathers, sisters, cousins and friends—they all turned out for the blessed event. For a long uneasy moment, we stared at each other, unaware of what to say. JoAnn led the introductions, and I wanted to cry. These were the people who had been with Sophia this far through her life, and the ones who would say good-bye so soon. I didn't know what to say, and I certainly wondered what they were thinking. Did they hate us? Commend us? Wish they had never met us?

We did what came naturally and started talking about the previous day's flight and how Rebecca was doing in the other room. The tension eased quickly and peace settled upon us all. They greeted us warmly and with loving smiles; it felt good to be with them.

Rebecca made it known that she wanted to see me when I arrived, so I was whisked away with Scott to see her. I entered a dimly lit suite where she was hooked up to monitors and nurses talked in hushed tones around her. I tried to find the correct words to say but instead touched her hand and started to cry. I was helpless to her pain and desperately wanted to do something to help, even take her place if I could. She was doing all the work so that I would end up with the gift. Many feelings swirled in my head, like forcing Rebecca to keep the baby since she was the deserving one. But, as God's grace comes freely to those who are undeserving, we would get the baby.

I stayed as long as I could and hoped she would invite me to stay during the delivery. Maybe she wanted me to ask, I don't know. I returned to the waiting room and encouraged everyone there of her progress. By this time, my sister and Regi were down on the floor playing cards with one of Rebecca's sisters. Unbelievably, they were laughing. How sweet it was that we could share the most special moment of all our lives together. We took videos, spoke about things like hair products and baby pictures, and took turns pacing. Every now and then someone crept down the corridor to listen at Rebecca's room in hopes they could report back with the news.

Almost uneventfully, word trickled in that Sophia had been born. I half expected Scott to come bounding down the hallway shouting the news, but I understood why he hadn't. He just said hello to the little girl he would shortly say good-bye to. Over the speaker we heard Brahm's "Lullaby," the hospital's way of celebrating the birth of Sophia Renee Stone.

At once, we all gathered outside Rebecca's room in hopes of catching a glimpse of Sophia. The curtains were drawn, and no one dared to open the door. We put our ear to the door, stooped to peek between the cracks in the curtains— anything to see what this special little girl looked like. Word had it that she was born at 4:06 p.m. weighing 7.5 pounds and stretching out to 20 inches long.

Finally, after about forty-five minutes, Scott pulled the curtain back and held up the tiny red-faced baby girl for everyone to see. At once, cameras clicked and flashes lit up the hallway. We got as close as we could to the window as two tiny blue eyes peered curiously at all the eager eyes gazing down at her. Here was the child I had prayed for, yearned for and dreamed about for more than eight years. I wanted to break the window and hold her, stroke the tiny wrinkles in her hands and whisper my long awaited "hello" into her ear. I longed to feel her brown hair and look into her eyes.

Everyone started crying, again. For Rebecca and Scott's family, tears for the times that wouldn't be, and us, for the times that were sure to come. We hugged each other, made light that we were all too softhearted and didn't dare leave the sight of this remarkable baby.

I realized, not for the first time, that this child was surrounded by more love on her first day of life than many children know in their whole lifetime.

The nurses told us Sophia wouldn't be ready for us for another two hours and that we should get something to eat while we could because we may not get out later. Hesitantly I agreed to leave, though I still had not gotten to touch or hold the baby. The hospital graciously allowed my sister, Regi and I to stay the night in an empty room since I would have to be on hand to nurse Sophia. They promised she wouldn't get fed and would wait on me. I knew that Scott and Rebecca needed this time together with Sophia, so we left.

We arrived back at the hospital in perfect timing. The nurses all said the baby was getting hungry. Now was the time I had been pumping eight weeks for! JoAnn, Regi, Annalisa and I were led into another room where we held our breath until we could finally see her.

The nurse entered the room with Sophia wrapped snugly in a blanket and lying close to her chest. All eyes turned to me instinctively as I held out my arms for my daughter. I had never held a baby so small but my arms became an instant cradle for this tiny body. She was helpless, yet my arms gave her strength. I kissed and stroked her face and whispered that her mommy loved her so much.

After we took turns holding her, the nurse sat me down and helped me through the steps of nursing. Everything I expected to happen at that moment did. Fireworks, sirens, whistles. She latched onto me naturally, even though I fumbled at every turn. Thank goodness for the nurse—at least someone knew what she was doing. We lasted for about thirty minutes, and then Sophia was asleep. Success. The eight long weeks of rigorous pumping, taking hormones and watching what I ate paid off. I was feeding my daughter.

143

That evening was spent shuffling Sophia between rooms. Scott and Rebecca were gracious to let us have equal time with her and even suggested that Sophia stay in the hospital room with us. I was elated that we would spend the first night with her. There we were—Sophia in her portable bed, me in the hospital bed, and Regi and Annalisa on uncomfortable fold-out lounge chairs. Not quite the Hyatt Regency! Little did we know that we were in for the night of our lives.

Once Sophia had been fed again, we were ready

to call it a night. Sheer exhaustion coursed through our veins. The day played heavily on our emotions, and that was as draining as a day on the jogging track. The phone line in our room stayed busy with family and friends calling and returning calls to us. I needed some rest.

With everyone tucked in bed, the three of us talked about the events of that day. We shared sentiments of how wonderfully Scott and Rebecca were handling the transition. Tomorrow we would appear before a judge with JoAnn's husband, Richard, to get a temporary stay of custody enabling us to have Sophia with us this week. At that point, we would only have to wait for the final papers stating that we were free to leave and return to Tennessee.

Though talk tapered off, sleep never came. Not for me anyway. Sophia was right next to me, and I couldn't help but hear every noise that came from her tiny mouth. I thought babies this young didn't make any sounds. I was wrong! I worried if she breathed too loudly, then I worried if she breathed too softly. I knew I was in the safest place possible, but I was also concerned about...well, everything. During the times I couldn't hear anything, I rolled to the side of the bed and placed my ear close enough to hear her miniature breaths. Other times I placed my hand on her chest to ensure it was moving up and down. When I wasn't touching her, a nurse would check her vital signs and assure me that everything was fine. We woke her every two to three hours to eat, whether she wanted to or not.

Morning found us with puffy, bloodshot eyes. Sophia slept fine however! The shuffling between rooms began again, which gave us time to shower and get prepared for the day. Scott, Rebecca and their families wanted to spend as much time with her as possible since they would both be released today. By now the papers that relinquished the baby to us were signed. I could withhold Sophia from them, but I never thought twice about that. They deserved this time, and I wasn't about to take it from them.

Whenever friends or family of Rebecca's or Scott's showed up, they came to get Sophia to show her off. Whenever she needed to be fed, she was brought back to my room. The day included shots, baby pictures and lots of diaper changing. Sophia held up well and hardly ever cried. She was bright-eyed and full of wonder at the world.

By mid-afternoon, we left the hospital to appear before a judge. The proceeding was simple and to the point, and we left with a hearty congratulation. Sophia was ours to take home from the hospital, and we had legal custody of her for the week while we awaited the papers from Tennessee allowing us to cross state lines with her. For the first time I felt like she was really ours. I wanted to rush back and take her for myself and never let her go. I am embarrassed to say that when I got back to the hospital and the shuffling started again, I wanted to put my foot down and keep her confined to my arms, my room. But I didn't.

During the time she spent with Scott and Rebecca, I waited patiently, knowing she would be hungry before long. That was my saving grace. Every time she came back to me, it was as though I hadn't seen her in days. I continued fumbling around with nursing, unsure each time whether she was getting enough or not. She usually spit up, which the nurse said meant she was getting plenty. Maybe even too much! My milk supply was actually fuller than most new mother's since I had been pumping for so long.

As the day wore on we got word that Rebecca and Sophia were going to be released soon. We were going home! We spent the last remaining hours visiting with Rebecca in her room, taking pictures and talking with everyone. Rebecca cradled Sophia, not saying much, gazing at her as if to study her features so she would never forget them.

We left the room so Rebecca could prepare to be released. On the way back to our room, Regi told me he had spoken with Scott earlier and they had one last request. Rebecca wanted to be wheeled out holding Sophia. Until then I assumed I would be the one to take her out. Instead, I conceded on this last request.

Excitement grew as we counted down the minutes until we left. Once back at the apartment, we would have Sophia all to ourselves. No more shuffling. No more nurses poking and prodding. No one to help me. The finality of leaving the well-trained nurses sunk in at once, and I felt my heart skip a beat that this helpless baby would be in the care of a helpless mommy! How was I to know what to do? I had plenty of people around me to help, but still I was nervous.

We packed everything up, dressed Sophia in a cute outfit and sent her down the hall to Rebecca's room. I watched her go from me for the last time and knew that soon she would be going home with us.

147

Annalisa and one of Rebecca's sisters went downstairs to videotape us all leaving together. When we were given final word, we grabbed our stuff and headed out. First out was me, JoAnn and Regi, carrying armloads of stuff from our stay. We waited at the end of the corridor to see Scott, Rebecca, Sophia, and their friends and family come down the hallway. When they rounded the corner, it was like an entourage! Everyone gathered around Rebecca and Sophia as they were escorted by wheelchair out of the hospital. Regi brought the car around, car seat in place, and we all milled around waiting for the right moment. We gave the family space and privacy to say their good-byes, which included many tears. We watched as they took turns holding Sophia, kissing her and whispering "I love you" into her ear, hoping it would be a moment she would always remember.

Regi and I stood by the car, allowing them to approach us when they were ready. Rebecca and Scott walked over, holding the baby close. I fought tears, trying to be strong yet overflowing with joy, love and gratefulness for these two brave teenagers. I thought Rebecca would place Sophia in my arms but instead she handed the baby to Regi, who placed her into the car seat. I reached for Rebecca and hugged her, wishing I could do so much more. We embraced for what seemed like forever and cried on each other's shoulder. How do you adequately thank a hero?

Just four months prior to this day, I felt hopeless to ever becoming a mother. Then in an instant these two teenagers were placed into our lives and made a decision that changed it all. First they chose life for their child, and then they chose us to be the parents. A divine appointment from God.

We said our good-byes, a moment that had to come, and piled into our respective vehicles. Rebecca's van followed us for what seemed like the whole way home, and I watched her stare at us through the window. She repeatedly wiped tears, and I didn't know whether to glance her way or not. I wanted her to find comfort from God for all her emotions. Did she have second thoughts now that it was over? Was she ready to forego her future plans and become a mommy? What could possibly go through the mind of a girl as she watched her baby fade into the sunset?

We finally arrived at the apartment, eager to show off our baby for the first official time. Once in the house, we all looked at each other as if to say, "What next?" There were no nurses to remind me to feed Sophia or to help me do whatever a mother is supposed to do. We waited for Sophia to signify she needed something with her tiny whimper, but otherwise went about our business.

149

That night we got up whenever Sophia made a sound. She woke up about every three hours, and I got up every hour. The new-mommy jitters followed me home from the hospital. I reminded myself that I once looked forward to these sleepless nights and intended to savor them as best I could.

July 7, 1998

Every day this mommy business gets a little easier. I know it will be simpler when I am back in my own home with Sophia's crib, swing, rocking chair and everything else that is lying in wait.

Today we got out for our first excursion. With the baby bundled and the diaper bag full of necessities, we did a little shopping. Everyone remarked on our adorable baby and then offered the comments I'd been waiting for: "You look great for just having a baby!" I smiled—beamed is more like it—and accepted the thanks without volunteering the facts. I didn't think people would ever ask if Sophia was adopted, but I never thought I could pass her off as being my child, as if a permanent sign would be attached that said, "Baby Adopted."

Once we got home Annalisa and I gave Sophia a sponge bath. She cried the whole time, mostly because I was too slow and meticulous, and I think she got cold. It broke my heart to hear her upset. As soon as we were done, I held her close and her sobs gently died down. I'm sure she already knows my touch and smell and is comforted by me. I wouldn't trade these feelings for anything in the world!

July 10, 1998

Word finally came this afternoon that we could take our daughter home. I feel like I will really be her mommy when we leave this state and get home. I am anxious to start our life together.

Once it was official, we quickly gathered our

stuff together and caught the first flight out. A pediatrician saw Sophia before we left and assured us we could fly with her. I've heard many stories that you cannot fly with a newborn because the air pressure will hurt their ears. I've already discovered that everyone wants to pass along their advice and answers to anything I need to know. I listen politely, smile, thank them, then do it my own way. I am resigned to the idea that I will not do everything right these next few months or years even, but with God's help Regi and I will raise her the best we know how.

We walked into our home with a new joy and happiness. The picture was complete now. We sighed with relief to be back in our familiar surroundings. Our quest was fulfilled and all our hard work had paid off. The dog was curious and poked in as much as we allowed. We introduced Sophia to her room, to her crib with its beautiful lace borders, and smothered her face with kisses.

151

July 13, 1998

My outlook on life has changed drastically. The focus has shifted away from my desires and needs to those of this innocent child. My dreams suddenly include an extra person and seem much different. The colors captured in the evening sunsets are a bit more vibrant now that there is someone else to share them with. Within this one tiny soul, I finally comprehend what I was placed on this earth for. In our eight years of marriage, I have longed to find my place, my calling. I used to pray that I would discover some untapped talent within the walls of my heart that would make me a better wife, a better person, a better Christian. Nothing tangible ever surfaced, and I questioned God time and again as to why He wouldn't answer my plea.

Now I know what God had in store for me, what the waiting was all about. It has been over a week that I've basked in the wonder of my daughter's life and contemplated why we were chosen for her. All I can come up with is...just because. For all the years in question, my destiny was being prepared until Sophia came to us. A sense of calm overtakes my spirit for the first time in many years; I am complete and happy with who I am. While some people attain lofty educational degrees or scale tall mountains to fulfill their dreams, mine is made complete in a less pretentious way. It is far more important than any other rank that could be bestowed upon me, and while I've not worn this hat for very long, God's plan for my life is clear. I am at peace.

Sometimes the gifts God sends are little, even obscure for a moment. While the birth of a child is a miracle in itself, the affect that child has upon our lives can take a while to figure out. In the beginning there is not much to do except feed, change and hold them. At first I questioned the significance of that until the day came that only I could soothe my daughter's cry. If we abandoned Sophia tomorrow, she would die. She is dependent upon us not only for nutrition and physical needs, but also for the shaping of her life, and that is an awesome responsibility and privilege. We can choose to raise her with or without love. With or without God. With or without compassion.

My favorite moments with Sophia are our times alone, just her and I in the dimly lit nursery as I rock her to sleep. She rests on my chest; our tummies pressed together, our breathing in sync. Molded together as one we rest and dream about the days ahead of playing house, running along sandy beaches and counting shooting stars.

153

Looking back on my struggles, how vivid the days of pain are. The nights I cried out to God, sometimes feeling comfort, other times feeling nothing. There were moments I felt empty and out of sorts, like I would never know true peace. It is easy to see the rainbow after the rain, but what about during the storm? There was no way to tell that our miracle was just around the corner, but what if I had given up and stopped praying or seeking the Lord? Only now do I see that giving up would have been easy; it was perseverance that took effort.

Hopeless situations seem just that—hopeless, devastating, consuming. Christians aren't exempt from these feelings, and that's okay. If you never experience the lowest points in life, you will never know what true joy is. That's a feeling you don't want to miss.

I still think about my abortion and possibly the only natural child I'll ever have. I've gotten beyond the sadness of losing that child and look forward to the day I'll see her in Heaven. I don't struggle with shame as before, nor do I dwell on what might have been. I revel in knowing the God of second chances! The concept of grace is so real to me. He picked up the brokenness of my life, put it back together and restored the gift of life to me. He is truly my Redeemer.

For now, I savor the moments when I gaze into the innocent eyes of this precious gift. I hold her and see love. I feel forgiveness. I feel abundance for a dream come true. But most of all, I see a promised fulfilled by a God who keeps His word. For that, I am grateful.

Epilogue

Abortion

Abortion has reached a staggering level in this country. One in four women have made that same trip to a hospital or clinic to "take care of the problem," only to leave with a greater burden in tow. The circumstances and feelings surrounding my abortion will never fade from my mind, and in a way I hope they never do. If I couldn't remember the torment I felt, I may never be able to prevent someone else from making that same mistake.

155

I believe the choice of abortion in a woman's life will not go without consequences. To what extent those consequences go is not for me to know. Whether physical or emotional problems, they lie in wait just below the surface of every other problem, watching for an opportune moment to grab hold of a fragile heart and condemn it to the point of thinking there is no forgiveness. How good it is to know we serve a God of second, third and fourth chances, a God whose mercy and grace covers all sin.

I chose to keep my abortion a secret from those who loved me most. In hindsight, I see that those very people I wanted to shield from my sin are the ones who have loved me more in spite of my weaknesses. The lie that Satan puts into our heads is that nobody will understand our crisis or forgive us afterward. On the contrary, it is in those very critical moments that family and friends are the strongest. I wish I had told my husband about my abortion earlier in our relationship so we could have walked through the impending struggles together. Instead I chose to face the quiet times alone, cry by myself and fight through the anger with no one by my side. It was a painful place to be—especially when there were people around me who would have reached out to help had I only asked.

For women who struggle with the guilt and shame of abortion, there is help. Christian Crisis Pregnancy Centers are equipped to provide confidential and safe counseling. Many great Bible studies are available also, and some churches provide this type of ministry for women in need. While reading this book may encourage you, taking a step toward healing will be up to you. I assure you that there is great comfort in gathering with women who share this common grief. I encourage you to make that phone call or set up that appointment in order to start your healing today.

Infertility

Infertility affects thousands of women today.

The pain that comes with the inability to conceive is much like what I experienced after my abortion. Once again, the pain dug deep into my soul, greater than anything I had ever experienced. I carved out a small hole in my soul that became my place of refuge instead of allowing anyone to help. I was quick to blame my husband for abandoning me emotionally, though I chose to do nothing about it. I relied on him to know my thoughts and struggles, and when he couldn't figure out what I was feeling, I took it as a sign that he just didn't care. How wrong I was! Communication is vital when facing any dilemma in a marriage, and I wanted to think that our communication breakdown was one-sided. The times I hurt the most were times I should have sought solace with my husband, instead of building animosity toward him. The feelings of anger certainly did nothing to help matters. But isn't it amazing how God can take what seemed to be a hopeless situation and weave the most beautiful story out of it?

The only way to get through the loneliness of infertility is through such communication. Women are affected differently than men, but men seldom remain unaffected. I encourage anyone who is experiencing infertility to seek out or form a support group. Such groups can be a great source of help for sorting through your emotions and usually provide a tremendous wealth of information. You can forge your way through. There is a light at the end of this seemingly endless tunnel, and I promise it will be easier to see if someone is by your side.

Adoption

If you had told me I would eventually be an adoptive parent, I would not have given it a second thought. It was never an issue in my family, and I hardly knew anyone who had been adopted. I never gave adoption a serious consideration because I didn't know enough about it. If you are facing infertility, you owe it to yourself to get acquainted with the subject. It has been one of the most amazing journeys of our life as a couple, and the joy we felt the first time Sophia was handed to us could not have been any sweeter if we had conceived her naturally. It continues to boggle my mind to think that there are literally millions of "good people" out there who could have happily provided a good life for our precious baby, yet we were chosen.

If you are waiting for a miracle, no matter what your situation, I encourage you to use your waiting time to draw close to the Lord. By abandoning every aspect of your life to Him, He will gain complete control to act according to His will. When the loneliness and desperation lingers longer than you think you can withstand, He is with you. This is the best time to learn your greatest lessons about His faithfulness and love. Don't ever forget that as you face infertility, a scarred past or anything else that seems too difficult to tunnel through. God does supply our needs according to His will. And His will is indeed perfect and worth the wait!

Forget the former things; do not dwell on the past. See, I am doing a new thing!

Now it springs up; do you not perceive it? I am making a way in the desert and streams in the wasteland.

—Isaiah 43:18-19

159

I love the Lord, for he heard my voice; he heard my cry for mercy. Because he turned his ear to me, I will call on him as long as I live. The cords of death entangled me, the anguish of the grave came upon me; I was overcome by trouble and sorrow. Then I called on the name of the Lord: "O Lord, save me!" The Lord is gracious and righteous; our God is full of compassion. The Lord protects the simplehearted; when I was in great need, he saved me. Be at rest once more, O my soul, for the Lord has been good to you. For you, O Lord, have delivered my soul from death, my eyes from tears, my feet from stumbling, that I may walk before the Lord in the land of the living. I believed; therefore I said, "I am greatly afflicted." And

in my dismay I said, "All men are liars."
How can I repay the Lord for all his
goodness to me?

Psalm 116:1-12, NIV

160